The Art of Drama Teaching

Michael Fleming

David Fulton Publishers
London

To Christopher

David Fulton Publishers Ltd
Ormond House, 26-27 Boswell Street, London WC1N 3JD

First published in Great Britain by David Fulton Publishers 1997
Reprinted 1998

Note: The right of Michael Fleming to be identified as the author of this work has been asserted by him in accordance with the Copyright, Designs and Patents Act 1988.

Copyright © Michael Fleming

British Library Cataloguing in Publication Data
A catalogue record for this book is available from the British Library

ISBN 1–85346–458–9

Typeset by Sheila Knight
Printed in Great Britain by The Cromwell Press Ltd, Trowbridge, Wilts

Contents

Acknowledgements

The writers who have influenced this book are acknowledged in the Introduction. My wife Marianne gave considerable practical help with the text and without her support the book would not have been completed. I am grateful to Jill Evans and her wonderful Year 10/11 drama class at St John's R.C. Comprehensive School, Bishop Auckland who allowed me to trial some of the techniques. I owe thanks to John Owens and the staff at David Fulton Publishers for their professionalism and support.

Acknowledgement is made to the following for permission to use copyright material:

Three Sisters by Chekhov, translated by Michael Frayn, published by Methuen and *Top Girls* by Carol Churchill, published by Methuen reproduced by permission of Reed Consumer Books Ltd; *The Plough and the Stars* by Sean O'Casey reproduced by permission of Macmillan General Books; *Our Country's Good* by Timberlake Wertenbaker, *Hedda Gabler* by Henrik Ibsen adapted by Christopher Hampton, *Waiting for Godot* by Samuel Beckett, *Rosencrantz and Guildenstern* by Tom Stoppard, *Philadelphia, Here I Come!* by Brian Friel reproduced by permission of Faber and Faber Ltd; *Separate Tables* copyright (c) by Terence Rattigan by permission of Michael Imison Playwrights Ltd 28 Almeida Street, London N1 1TD; *Death of a Salesman* copyright (c) 1948, 1949, 1951, 1952 by Arthur Miller, renewed 1975, 1976, 1979, 1980 by Arthur Miller and *The Crucible* copyright (c) 1952, 1953, 1954 by Arthur Miller, renewed 1980, 1981, 1982 reproduced by permission of Greene and Heaton Limited; *The Royal Hunt of the Sun* by Peter Shaffer copyright (c) Peter Shaffer, 1964 and *The Theban Plays* by Sophocles, translated by E F Watling (Penguin Classics, 1947) copyright (c) E F Watling, 1947 reproduced by permission of Penguin Books Limited; *Talking Heads* by Alan Bennett first published by BBC books 1988 reprinted by permission of The Peters Fraser and Dunlop Group Limited on behalf of Alan Bennett (c) Forelake Ltd 1988; *A Man for All Seasons* by Robert Bolt, published by Heinemann Educational Books reproduced by permission of Heinemann Publishers Oxford; *Absurd Person Singular* by Alan Ayckbourn published by Chatto and Windus reproduced by permission of Random House U.K.Limited; *On Baile's Strand* by W. B.Yeats by permission of A. P. Watt Limited on behalf of Michael Yeats; *An Inspector Calls* by J. B. Priestley reprinted by permission of the Peters Fraser and Dunlop Group Limited on behalf of (c) 1945 J. B. Priestley; *Galileo* copyright (c) by Bertolt Brecht, 1952, by permission of Indiana University Press .

Introduction

To most people outside education, drama means reading and performing plays. In school, however, (particularly up to the age of 15–16) drama is more likely to involve various forms of role taking, dramatic play and improvisation rather than work from text. The extreme divisions between 'drama' and 'theatre' practice which were characteristic of the seventies and eighties have given way to a more inclusive view of the subject which sees a place for all manifestations of drama in schools. This book takes that view further by demonstrating that many of the strategies which can be used by drama teachers and pupils in the classroom have close affinities with the techniques used by playwrights in the construction of dramatic texts. By exploring the way those techniques are used by dramatists, insight can be gained into the nature of the art form which in turn will inform classroom teaching.

The book consists of a description of twenty-five 'topics', 'techniques' or 'conventions' and an exploration of the way these can be adapted and used by drama teachers and pupils. Although the book is intended to make a practical contribution to the teaching of drama, it also constitutes an argument and point of view about the nature of drama, the concept of drama as an art form and the idea of teaching drama itself as an art.

Teaching drama

In my previous book (*Starting Drama Teaching*, 1994) I discussed in some detail the polarisation and divisions which have beset the history of drama teaching in the last fifty years. I do not want to repeat that discussion in any great detail because the consensus which seemed to be emerging then is even more clearly established now. In countries like Canada and Australia where drama teaching has flourished in recent years these divisions were never felt as strongly. Publications on drama now largely take it for granted that the dichotomies between 'process' and 'product'; 'theatre' and 'drama'; 'drama for understanding' and 'drama as art'; 'experience' and 'performance' were false polarities.

Rather than re-examine the conflicting arguments and divisions which split the drama teaching world, I want to summarise some of the reasons for the consensus which has emerged:

1. There has been a recognition that opposition to theatre which was characteristic of the approach of some advocates of drama in education was in fact a rejection of one particular, traditional conception of theatre and theatre practice.

2. There has been an erosion of the distinction between 'experiencing' and 'spectating' by recognising that participants (or more appropriately, 'percipients') in drama are always spectators; there is an ongoing reflective element in drama which is part of its power as an art form.

3. There has been more acceptance of the fact that development in understanding in drama (including the use of drama across the curriculum) arises through participation in the art form: education *in* and *through* drama complement each other

4. There has been recognition that participation in drama develops and changes as pupils get older. Developmental models of the kind proposed by the Arts Council (1992) have been a helpful focus for discussion of such issues.

5. Writers like O'Toole (1992) and O'Neill (1995) who have advocated models of 'process' drama have, contrary to initial impressions, helped heal divisions because it is now easier to identify process drama as simply one genre, one manifestation of the art form amongst others which might be appropriate in schools.

6. There is less reliance on psychology and theories of child play for theoretical underpinning for classroom drama practice and a greater readiness to embrace the work of drama theoreticians such as Esslin, Elam, Pfister, Szondi and theatre practitioners such as Brecht and Boal.

7. There has been a gradual shift from a theoretical focus on the subjective, personal growth of the individual through creative processes of self-expression to a recognition of the social nature of drama and the importance of the development of understanding in objective, cultural contexts.

The fact that there has been an erosion of some of the divisions that have split the drama world in the past does not mean that there are now no disagreements in the field; that is to be welcomed because complete consensus would more likely signal intellectual atrophy than harmony. There has been welcome increase in research activity (Taylor, 1996), confirmed by the arrival of a new research journal, *Research in Drama Education*, for the exchange of ideas. Amongst some of the issues which are still unresolved, disagreement centres on whether it is appropriate to focus on the teaching of drama skills and whether a satisfactory account of progression in drama can be provided (Hornbrook, 1995).

Traditionally, writers on drama in education have been suspicious of the concept of skills in drama because of the dangers of defining them too narrowly. Talk of skills was resisted because of the implied emphasis on decontextualised theatre skills (acting, stage design, etc.) with insufficient emphasis on content. In *Starting Drama Teaching* I suggested that the term 'competence' might be more appropriate to embrace the complex forms of knowledge and understanding which are needed in making and responding to drama. The important point to emphasise is that developing ability in drama need not and should not entail a focus on narrowly defined skills devoid of recognition of the importance of content and context; the precise terminology is less important.

It is against this background of growing consensus and unresolved issues that this book has been conceived and written. It is intended to support teachers and pupils in their work in the classroom as well as to make a contribution to developing ideas on the acquisition of ability in drama.

Drama as art

One of the significant insights of drama education theorists was the recognition that, left to their own devices, children are unlikely to create drama of any depth which will further their understanding of human situations. This view marked a departure from earlier practitioners who based their work on the efficacy of unfettered child play. The solution offered which changed the emphasis from pure play, was for the teacher to intervene and take over responsibility for the creation of drama. That approach still tends to persist; it is for the teacher to provide significant content and artistic form. A deceptively simple alternative would have been to teach the pupils how to do the same.

Stated that baldly, the suggestion is an oversimplification because it fails to recognise that the degree of teacher intervention necessary in creating the drama will vary with the age of the pupils. It also fails to acknowledge that teacher-led drama may be a way of tacitly improving pupils' own drama expertise. However, it is fair to say that in process drama and in many of the practical books which have been published in recent years, it is the teacher rather than the pupils who is acting as 'playwright', orchestrating the work and planning which conventions to use. 'Getting better at drama' has partly to do with an increasing skill in being able to take an idea and translate it into dramatic form; that ability is likely to be developed by examining the way dramatists do the same. It also has to do with gaining some insight, however implicitly, into the nature of the art form.

One of the ways pupils (and indeed teachers who are new to the subject) conceptualise drama is to see its purpose as replicating real experience. It is little wonder that such is the case because the form of drama which frequently dominates the conception of the art form is derived from the realism of film and television. This understanding of the way drama works was unwittingly reinforced by some of the early drama in education approaches which relied exclusively on 'living through' improvisations. These happened at life pace, had unknown outcomes and the meaning was negotiated during the process. Such experiences, when they worked well, provided an extraordinary degree of emotional engagement and excitement through their immediacy. However, because there was less explicit emphasis on *making* drama, the implicit message was to deny drama as an artificial, fictional 'construct'.

A fruitful way of thinking about dramatic art, then, is not to see it as merely replicating experience but to be aware of its potential to explore and examine experience in ways which would otherwise be denied to us in real life. 'Reality' comes under conscious control in drama. It works paradoxically by revealing complexities through simplification. By editing out some of the features which are characteristic of encounters in real life, aspects of behaviour can be thrown into relief. Many of the conventions which teachers use in drama such as tableau (freezing a moment in time) and hotseating (questioning characters in role) serve to slow the action down, to step out of 'real' time to explore experiences in more depth.

Examination of the art of the dramatist, then, is not just a practical source of ideas, but is a reminder of the degree to which dramatic art is a human construct. Of course customs have changed in the degree to which dramatists have seen naturalistic representation as their main goal. 'Alienation' techniques in the theatre are often considered a fairly modern phenomenon (associated with Brecht) but many plays (classical. medieval, renaissance) have had a dimension which can be described as 'meta-theatrical' self awareness. The fact that drama is 'unreal' is essential to the way it works as art, and the full implications of this have not always been appreciated in drama teaching.

A number of the plays which have been chosen to illustrate a particular convention also provide a more general insight into the nature of drama. For example, in Wilder's *Our Town* one of the characters is able to step back in time and gain a new perspective on her former life by revisiting it, almost as a spectator at a play. The fact that she is dead makes the convention all the more imaginative. Brecht's use of analogy in *Galileo* highlight's the play's central theme but also provides an insight into the way broad themes can be emphasised without denying the particularity of the art form (sub-plots function in the same way). Exploration of beginnings and endings highlights the nature of drama as a human construct and aesthetic experience; it does not have to reinforce traditional models of constructing plays (rising action, climax, catastrophe) but recognises that all drama has shape and structure. The same is true of the study of exposition. The convention of counterpoint illustrated by O'Casey's *The Plough and the Stars* draws attention to the extent to which meaning in drama does not have to be confined to a process of negotiation but can be a function of the juxtaposition of different elements in the work. Externalising inner conflict as exemplified in *Dr Faustus* highlights the way drama works dialectically (see Chapter 7).

A number of exponents have written on the nature of drama as an art form, emphasising such elements as its use of time and space, light and darkness and highlighting important ingredients such as tension and the use of constraint. I do not propose to attempt a definitive account of the nature of drama as art here, but to draw attention to those aspects which emerge most strongly from the choice of extracts and which may be useful to pupils and teachers when making or responding to drama. The conventions point to key overlapping elements of obliquity, concealment, distance and use of multi-levels.

Creating different levels of meaning in drama arises specifically through the use of irony (when the audience's perception extends beyond that of the participants) and through the use of framing action (when the meaning of what follows is changed by the initial actions). The use of false identity is an explicit example of concealment but is also an integral element of much drama. For example, successful exposition at the beginning of a play relies as much on what to conceal as on deciding what should be revealed. The use of minor characters to provide a perspective on events and the use of reported action are examples of the way drama can work obliquely. Conventions such as play within a play and off-stage action are ways of distancing the central action which of course is also a method of working obliquely.

The list of twenty-five 'conventions' or 'topics', then, is not intended to represent discrete categories. They are presented in separate chapters solely for the purpose of analysis. They are simply headings under which the art of drama is considered. In practice they overlap considerably and there are therefore a number of cross-references. Taken together they contribute to an understanding of drama as art.

Teaching drama as an art

Using the metaphor of art to apply to teaching is a useful corrective to the current tendency to see the process of teaching and learning exclusively in clinical, over-simplified terms. Precise targets, clear objectives, pre-determined learning outcomes and mechanical processes do not by themselves guarantee successful teaching. Any engagement with human beings which is intended to bring about learning is of necessity a subtle and fairly uncertain process. However, I do not intend this to be a diatribe against rigour and focus in favour of a romantic celebration of *laissez faire* approaches; I have seen too many teachers and student teachers benefit in their work from specification of clear targets and goals. The key is to recognise that in any teaching, no matter how focused the learning objectives, it is important not to lose sight of the fact that it is above all a human enterprise which demands sensitivity to the way participants are responding and engaging with the context.

If that is true of teaching in general, it is even more true of drama. Drama teaching is an art in that it does not lend itself to the mechanical application of methods and techniques. Sensitivity to contexts is essential. One of the purposes of this book is to deepen understanding of the rich rather than mechanised use of drama conventions by describing their use in play texts. Drama teaching is also an art in that it demands the appropriate selection and employment of artistic form to create meaning. It is an argument of this book that teaching drama is also about enabling pupils to do likewise.

Aims

A number of writers have had an influence on this book. The idea came from David Lodge's excellent publication, *The Art of Fiction,* in which he takes a number of topics and relates these to selected extracts from novels.

As one would expect from a writer like Lodge, the theoretical under-pinning drawn from literary theory is considerable but it never weighs heavily; he writes in this book with a light and accessible touch which is most engaging. Neelands's book, *Structuring Drama Work*, which describes numerous dramatic conventions convinced me of the value of using a handbook format. This book and publications like Morgan and Saxton's *Teaching Drama,* which also lists and describes conventions, did much to demystify drama teaching. As well as introducing new ideas, both books helped make some of the work of Heathcote available to teachers. I was near completion of the project when I read O'Neill's, *Drama Worlds* and was encouraged on two counts: the fact that she was making similar connections convinced me that I was working on the right lines; I was also pleased that the differences in approach and intention meant that there was little overlap. I have included references to those publications where appropriate which I hope the reader will find helpful. Kempe has been one of the writers on drama who has kept play texts to the fore and I have always found his work stimulating. O'Toole is perhaps better known now for *The Process of Drama* but he, with Haseman, linked drama teaching techniques with play texts in *Dramawise*. Those writers, amongst others, have been influential in different ways but it is to the writings of Bolton which I have found myself returning again and again for inspiration; I particularly admire the way in which he is able to combine theory and practice so successfully.

In writing the book I have attempted to achieve a number of aims:

- to provide a variety of topics or techniques to be used and addressed in the classroom either as free-standing exercises or incorporated into drama projects, and to deepen understanding of those techniques by illustrating their use in play texts;
- to contribute to the debate about skills and progress by illustrating ways in which pupils can actually be taught drama;
- to provide a collection of extracts which can serve to illustrate the topic but which can also be used in the classroom in their own right;
- to further demonstrate the relationship between drama in education and theatre traditions as a way of supporting the consensus which has emerged;
- to provide further insight into drama as art;
- to provide a resource for in-service work and the training of teachers.

I suspect that the book will have most immediate appeal to teachers of older pupils. Certainly the extracts from plays are more suitable to older age groups. However, many of the conventions are appropriate for use with younger pupils, as a number of the examples indicate. For instance, a lesson with five/six year olds taught by Bolton (1992: 81) based on the Nativity could be described in terms of a number of topics addressed in the book. At the start of the drama, the teacher in role enters as a weary Joseph supporting Mary (framing action); he speaks, 'It's all right my dear, I'm sure we'll find somewhere to stay the night . . .' (the dialogue as a form of beginning and exposition sets the context); a scarf is used to represent the baby (this use of an object focuses the action); the pupils have to demonstrate that they are capable of looking after a baby (they use mime to do so); when they succeed, the teacher tells the story of the birth of Jesus (using narration); they name the baby and sing (using ritual as an appropriate ending).

When choosing examples of lessons and dramatic activities I have deliberately drawn on the work of published practitioners as well as on my own experience to illustrate a wide variety of approaches. Although the book as a whole is intended to provide insight into the art of drama teaching, it is reasonable to expect that readers will dip into it selectively. I have tried to follow a similar format for each chapter so that (apart from the cross-references) each section can be read separately. Where possible, I have tried to choose extracts from familiar texts, and to represent a selection of dramatic styles and periods. The selected headings fall into three categories:

1. techniques which are familiar to drama in education practitioners (into which I hope new insights are provided)
2. more traditional topics which have tended to be overlooked
3. some new suggestions.

I chose not to group them in this way, nor to present the extracts chronologically or in some kind of logical sequence (by starting with beginnings and proceeding to endings). Paradoxically, the arbitrary sequence of an alphabetical list highlights the organic nature of the relationships between the chapters better than any attempt at rational grouping. Just as art simplifies in order to reveal complexities, the artificial categories in the book are intended to provide an insight into the art of drama teaching.

CHAPTER ONE

Alternative Perspective

INSPECTOR: Mr Birling?

BIRLING: Yes. Sit down, Inspector.

INSPECTOR: Thank you, sir.

Edna takes the Inspector's hat and coat and goes out

BIRLING: Have a glass of port – or a little whisky.

INSPECTOR: No, thank you, Mr Birling. I'm on duty. (*He turns the desk chair a little away from the desk and sits*)

BIRLING: You're new, aren't you?

INSPECTOR: Yes, sir. Only recently transferred.

BIRLING: I thought you must be. I was an alderman for years – and Lord Mayor two years ago – and I'm still on the Bench – so I know the Brumley police officers pretty well – and I thought I'd never seen you before. (*He sits L. of the table*)

INSPECTOR: Quite so.

BIRLING: Well, what can I do for you? Some trouble about a warrant?

INSPECTOR: No, Mr Birling.

BIRLING: (*after a pause, with a touch of impatience*) Well, what is it then?

INSPECTOR: I'd like some information, if you don't mind, Mr Birling. Two hours ago a young woman died in the Infirmary. She'd been taken there this afternoon because she'd swallowed a lot of strong disinfectant. Burnt her inside out, of course.

ERIC: (*involuntarily*) My God!

INSPECTOR: Yes, she was in great agony. They did everything they could for her at the Infirmary, but she died. Suicide of course.

BIRLING: (*rather impatiently*) Yes, yes. Horrible business. But I don't understand why you should come here, Inspector –

INSPECTOR: (*cutting through, massively*) I've been round to the room she had, and she left a letter there and a sort of diary. Like a lot of these young women who get into various kinds of trouble, she'd used more than one name. But her original name – her real name – was Eva Smith.

BIRLING: (*thoughtfully*) Eva Smith?

INSPECTOR: Do you remember her, Mr Birling?

BIRLING: (*slowly*) No – I seem to remember hearing that name – Eva Smith – somewhere. But it doesn't convey anything to me. And I don't see where I come into this.

INSPECTOR: She was employed in your works at one time.

BIRLING: Oh – that's it, is it? Well, we've several hundred young women there, y'know, and they keep changing.

INSPECTOR: (*rising*) This young woman, Eva Smith, was a bit out of the ordinary. I found a photograph of her in her lodgings. Perhaps you'd remember her from that. (*He takes a photograph about postcard size out of his pocket and moves towards Birling*)

Gerald rises and moves about the table to look over Birling's shoulder. Eric rises and moves below the table to see the photograph. The Inspector quickly moves above Birling and prevents both of them from seeing it. They are surprised and rather annoyed. Birling stares hard and with recognition at the photograph, which the Inspector then takes from him and replaces in his pocket, as he moves down L.C.

GERALD: (*following the Inspector down; showing annoyance*) Any particular reason why I shouldn't see this girl's photograph, Inspector?

INSPECTOR: (*moving to the desk*) There might be.

ERIC: And the same applies to me, I suppose?

INSPECTOR: Yes.

GERALD: I can't imagine what it could be.

ERIC: Neither can I. (*He sits below the table*)

BIRLING: And I must say, I agree with them, Inspector.

J. B. Priestley, *An Inspector Calls*

Commentary

The arrival of the inspector at the Birling household near the beginning of Act One interrupts the dinner being held to celebrate an engagement. The inspector's persistent questioning as the play develops disturbs the surface order and stability of the family depicted in the initial scene and challenges their sense of moral duty and responsibility. It is gradually revealed that each member of the family not only knew Eva, the girl whose suicide is reported in this extract, but also contributed in some way to her death. Birling sacked her from his factory for being one of the ringleaders in a strike for more pay; Sheila, his daughter, unjustly used her position of social influence and power to cause the girl to lose her job as a shop assistant; Mrs Birling, as a prominent member of a charity organisation, refused financial help when Eva was in desperate need; Eric, the son, took advantage of the girl and made her pregnant. Even Gerald, Sheila's fiancé, turns out to have had an affair with Eva. The chain of events brought her to a state of desperation and eventual suicide. Each of the incidents exposes an aspect of the dubious morality lying below the outward veneer of decorum, respectability and righteousness: deception, snobbishness, jealousy and self-centredness are displayed in different measures by the various members of the family. An alternative perspective is revealed to the audience and, to some degree, to the characters themselves as the truth is uncovered.

This extract is typical of the highly naturalistic style and content of most of the play. The inspector, true to type, refuses a drink on duty and is single-minded in his questioning. He emphasises the awful manner of the girl's death as he does several times throughout the play. The audience is here given a hint that the girl might have been connected with more than one member of the family; the truth of this is confirmed as the play develops. The diary and letter provide the rationale for the inspector's obvious knowledge of the truth and contribute to the realistic depiction of events. The use of the photograph is also important for the structure of the play – it is necessary that each family member recognises the girl's photograph separately so that the truth can emerge gradually.

The play's development centres on the shift of perspective which reveals the truth about the family: their involvement in the particular events of the girl's life and the underlying morality and ideology which determine their actions. The moral force of the play is strengthened when the identity of the inspector becomes more ambiguous towards the end. When the family receive confirmation that Inspector Goole is not known to the local police force they start to give different interpretations of the events: that the whole affair might be a hoax, that it was not necessarily the same girl in each case (the inspector could have been using different photographs), that perhaps there was no dead body at all. The self-deception underlines the moral bankruptcy of several of the characters; they are unable to see that their actions were wrong irrespective of whether there was one girl or several. Only Sheila shows awareness of that fact.

It is the departure from naturalism, the use of time shift and the ambiguity which surrounds the identity of the inspector, which causes the significant change in perspective which underlines the central moral theme. The play ends with a telephone announcement to the Birlings that the body of a girl has been found and an inspector will shortly arrive to question them. It is as if time has been suspended for the duration of the play. The family had momentarily thought that they had escaped from the consequences of their actions.

It is also the departure from naturalism which provides a key to the alternative perspective in Thornton Wilder's *Our Town*. The play depicts very ordinary events in the lives of the characters in a New Hampshire town. In the third and final act the author uses a bold and imaginative convention: Emily, who has died in childbirth, is allowed to return to an earlier time in her life (her birthday when she was twelve years old) to experience it now from the perspective of one who has died.

The convention of letting Emily return to her former life works because of the epic style in which the play as a whole was conceived and written. The Stage Manager is a key figure in the play, commenting on the action, interacting with the characters and orchestrating the events. He has the power not only to reach back in time and bring the past into the present, but also to allow Emily to live her life and 'watch herself living it'. This allows her to have an alternative perspective on the events of her life. Emily is now able to perceive that people simply do not live their lives with intensity. It is not that there is any revelation of cruelty or injustice in what she sees: on the contrary, the family birthday scene is generous and loving. What Emily finds hard to bear is the blandness, emotional restraint and lack of real connections between people.

The process of providing an alternative perspective on events can be seen both as a specific approach to drama and as a function of art and drama as a whole. It is therefore a suitable topic with which to begin this account of dramatic conventions. The way Wilder uses alternative perspective in *Our Town* can be seen as a metaphor for the way in which the dramatic art process works. It is as if Emily is watching a performance as spectator and participating in it at the same time. Life and the way it is normally lived is thereby subject to fresh scrutiny. Emily's utterance when she returns to her former life, 'So all that was going on and we never noticed', is not at all inappropriate as an insight into the power of drama as an art form. Similarly her comment about life, 'It goes so fast', is also pertinent. Drama frequently works by slowing action down in order to explore experiences in more depth.

Examples

Alternative perspective is described in this chapter as a convention in its own right, but it is also one of the underlying purposes for many of the other techniques which will be described in this book. Reporting events, irony, unspoken thoughts and counterpoint are all conventions which can be used in order to provide a different perspective on the action of the drama. By consciously seeking to provide contrasting views, the teacher can develop in the participants an insight into the fact that events are always subject to alternative constructions and reinterpretations.

Just as a fresh perspective is thrown on a family in *An Inspector Calls* and on a simple domestic scene in *Our Town*, virtually any drama can be given more depth by juxtaposing a contrasting view of the events which are unfolding. There are a number of ways in which an alternative perspective can be provided in the course of creating a drama:

• two versions of the same event are created;

  A Head of House is interviewing two pupils to get to the bottom of some misdemeanour (perhaps a fight or a broken window). Two versions of how things happened are enacted from the different perspectives of the pupils involved. The simplest approach and the way the pupils are likely to interpret the task is to reveal how one is telling the truth, the other lying. More subtly, the two versions can be shown which both pupils genuinely believe to be true.

• a diary entry or letter is juxtaposed against the enacted scene;

  In a play about an expedition to uncharted territory, the leader of the expedition reads aloud reflections on the events of the day in the form of a diary or letter home. This technique is fairly common in the drama literature as a form of summary (see Chapter 16: Narration) but it is used here either to show the leader's self-deception or to inject tension if the intention is actually to deceive.

• a reported version of an event is followed by an enactment of how things actually were;

  The report of a first date to a friend is set against the way things were actually experienced. Here the emphasis is on blatant exaggeration and distortion rather than self-deception and the potential for humour is strong. A similar contrast can be achieved if a married man describes the nature of his relationship with his wife to his chauvinist friends at work in a version which is very different from the reality.

• the way events were experienced is contrasted with a dream sequence showing how the protagonist wished they could have been;

13

In a play about an estranged mother and daughter, the meeting which achieves very little and was full of embarrassing silences is followed by the dream version of how the participants wished things could have been.

- a newspaper article is contrasted with the truth of what actually happened;

The account of a crime which describes the perpetrator as callous and calculating is contrasted with scenes which depict the circumstances which drove the individual to commit the crime and hint at the mixed feelings and troubled consciences of those involved.

- the arrival of a stranger changes the perception of events;

A family gathering is interrupted by the arrival of a character who gradually provides an alternative perspective on the scene which is depicted, similar to the technique used in *An Inspector Calls.* For example, it is revealed that one of the family has hidden a criminal past.

It is significant that in many of the practical approaches described above the dramatic tension is generated not purely from within the particular scene but by virtue of its contrast with the source of the other perspective, whether this be through writing, commentary, enacted scene or other means. The total meaning of the drama is derived from the juxtaposition of two versions of events which allows the individual scenes to be fairly simple and ordinary. There is thus a pragmatic as well as an aesthetic reason for using this technique because in its simplest form it is very accessible to pupils.

The examples given are suitable for more experienced, older participants in drama. The lesson described below was planned for a younger, less experienced class but is nevertheless based on the same idea of providing alternative perspectives on events. There are tensions involved in the notion of progression in drama. Approaches to teaching the subject which start with 'basics' run the risk of having pupils engaged in endless tasks such as miming exercises with little focus on meaning. On the other hand it was suggested that, despite young children's natural capacity for dramatic play, the notion of helping pupils to acquire skills in drama needs to be taken seriously and progression needs to be built into a drama syllabus. The following lesson was planned for a Year 7 class at a very early stage in a drama course and the work which is controlled and directed is intended to provide maximum security for the teacher as well as easily achievable goals for the pupils.

Lesson sequence

1. The class play the 'keys of the kingdom' game. One pupil sits blindfold in a chair and tries to capture other pupils as they attempt to steal a bunch of keys. (Fleming, 1994: 73).

2. They are asked to imagine possible real life situations in which someone might be attempting to steal keys in order to escape; this might eventually lead to a newspaper headline such as 'DARING ESCAPE FOILS CAPTORS'. In groups of four they enact a scene largely using mime with just one or two whispered exchanges in which they make their escape while the guard sleeps.

3. The scene is repeated but this time the context is explained by the addition of one or two lines taken from the journal of one of the escapees, e.g. 'We have decided that tonight is the night we must try our escape. We cannot rely on the police to find us and we know that we are not going to be released. If the guard wakes the consequences will be severe but we have to try . . .'

4. This time the scene is enacted again but one of the group has second thoughts and does not want to go through with the escape. The others finally succeed in their attempts at persuasion.

Commentary

The game requires silence and stealth. It creates an appropriate atmosphere for the drama which follows.

Because the drama is working only at the level of external action the challenge in this exercise is not high. It is controlled yet motivating. The language demands are minimal but they are also manageable for an inexperienced class.

This short group writing task allows the pupils to have more ownership of the scene without taxing their ability to structure a dramatic plot. The exercise helps the pupils begin to internalise the action as they start to think a little more about the context.

Here an extra element of dramatic tension is built into the scene. Notice that the outcome is predetermined by the teacher. There is no attempt to engage in 'living through' dramatic playing whereby the outcome is determined spontaneously.

15

Lesson sequence	**Commentary**
5. The scenes may now be shared with the whole class. The scenes are preceded by the 'reading' of a newspaper article invented by the teacher which describes the extreme heroism of one of the escapees who master-minded and led the escape. It is the same one who in reality almost jeopardised the plan at the last minute. The teacher needs to give some indication to the class of what to expect, 'Surprisingly, when the story appeared in the papers some time after the escape, the version there was rather different . . .'	The scenes have been reasonably well 'rehearsed' and because the demands are not too high they can be shared with some sense of achievement. The reading of the newspaper article should not come as a surprise to the pupils. They should know that the version in the newspaper will be different.
6. The class are asked to speculate on how the false information was acquired, whether the person involved would want to put the record straight, how the other captives might feel, whether they would take any action, and so on.	Here the thought-provoking element comes from outside rather than from within the drama itself. This is appropriate for a drama activity at an early stage in a course designed to provide achievable and satisfying goals.

CHAPTER TWO

Analogy

Before a little Italian customs house early in the morning. ANDREA *sits upon one of his traveling trunks at the barrier and reads Galileo's book. The window of a small house is still lit, and a big grotesque shadow like an old witch and her cauldron, falls upon the house wall beyond. Barefoot* CHILDREN *in rags see it and point to the little house.*

CHILDREN (*singing*):
  One, two, three, four, five, six,
  Old Marina is a witch.
  At night, on a broomstick she sits
  And on the church steeple she spits.

CUSTOMS OFFICER (*to* ANDREA): Why are you making this journey?

ANDREA: I am a scholar.

CUSTOMS OFFICER (*to his* CLERK): Put down under 'Reason for Leaving the Country': Scholar. (*He points to the baggage:*) Books! Anything dangerous in these books?

ANDREA: What is dangerous?

CUSTOMS OFFICER: Religion. Politics.

ANDREA: These are nothing but mathematical formulas.

CUSTOMS OFFICER: What's that?

ANDREA: Figures.

CUSTOMS OFFICER: Oh, figures. No harm in figures. Just wait a minute, sir, we will soon have your papers stamped. (*He exits with* CLERK.)

Meanwhile, a little council of war among the children has taken place. ANDREA *quietly watches. One of the* BOYS, *pushed forward by the others, creeps up to the little house from which the shadow comes, and takes the jug of milk in the doorstep.*

ANDREA (*quietly*): What are you doing with that milk?

BOY (*stopping in mid-movement*): She is a witch.

17

The other CHILDREN *run away behind the customs house. One of them shouts, 'Run, Paolo!'*

ANDREA: Hmm! And because she is a witch she mustn't have milk. Is that the idea?

BOY: Yes.

ANDREA: And how do you know she is a witch?

BOY (*points to shadow on house wall*): Look!

ANDREA: Oh! I see.

BOY: And she rides on a broomstick at night – and she bewitches the coachman's horses. My cousin Luigi looked through the hole in the stable roof, that the snow storm made, and heard the horses coughing something terrible.

ANDREA: Oh! How big was the hole in the stable roof?

BOY: Luigi didn't tell. Why?

ANDREA: I was asking because maybe the horses got sick because it was cold in the stable. You had better ask Luigi how big that hole is.

BOY: You are not going to say Old Marina isn't a witch because you can't.

ANDREA: No, I can't say she isn't a witch. I haven't looked into it. A man can't know about a thing he hasn't looked into, or can he?

BOY: No! But THAT! (*He points to the shadow.*) She is stirring hellbroth.

ANDREA: Let's see. Do you want to have a look? I can lift you up.

BOY: You lift me to the window mister! (*He takes a sling-shot out of his pocket.*) I can really bash her from there.

ANDREA: Hadn't we better make sure she is a witch before we shoot? I'll hold that.

The BOY *puts the milk jug down and follows him reluctantly to the window.* ANDREA *lifts the boy up so that he can look in.*

ANDREA: What do you see?

BOY (*slowly*): Just an old girl cooking porridge.

ANDREA: Oh! Nothing to it then. Now look at her shadow, Paolo.

The BOY *looks over his shoulder and back and compares the reality and the shadow.*

BOY: The big thing is a soup ladle.

ANDREA: Ah! A ladle! You see, I would have taken it for a broomstick, but I haven't looked into the matter as you have, Paolo. Here is your sling.

CUSTOMS OFFICER (*returning with the* CLERK *and handling* ANDREA *his papers*): All present and correct. Good luck, sir.

ANDREA *goes, reading Galileo's book. The* CLERK *starts to bring his baggage after him. The barrier rises.* ANDREA *passes through, still reading the book. The* BOY *kicks over the milk jug.*

BOY (*shouting after* ANDREA): She *is* a witch! She *is* a witch!
ANDREA: You saw with your own eyes: think it over!

The BOY *joins the others. They sing:*

> One, two, three, four, five, six
> Old Marina is a witch.
> At night, on a broomstick she sits
> And on the church steeple she spits.

Bertolt Brecht, Galileo

Commentary

Galileo's last act of the play, in the scene which precedes this one, is to hand over to his assistant Andrea a book he has been secretly writing. In this, the last scene of the play, Andrea is smuggling the book out of the country. However most of the action is focused on the children playing in the street, an incident which seems in the context of the play to be a mere diversion; they have not previously been part of the action. The children are convinced that the occupant of one of the houses is a witch because they mistake the shadow of a soup ladle which she is using for a broomstick. They persist in their belief even though Paolo, one of the boys, is shown evidence to the contrary by being lifted up to look over the wall. This final scene is dramatically effective because, far from being irrelevant, it acts as an analogy for the central theme of the play as a whole.

The simple self-contained incident with the children replicates the refusal of Galileo's contemporaries to believe the evidence of what he presented to them. His challenge to traditional beliefs that the earth is the centre of the universe was such an affront to established religious authority that Galileo was tried by the Inquisition in Rome. He does in fact recant his belief, much to the disappointment of his assistant Andrea who refuses to accept that Galileo did so for ignoble reasons. Andrea wants to believe that it was not fear of punishment which motivated Galileo, but that his actions were part of an overall plan to ensure the survival of his work which is eventually smuggled out of the country in this scene. One of the themes of the play, that people are inclined to believe what they want to believe, manifests itself in different ways: the inquisitors deny the evidence which is presented to them; Andrea persists in his faith in the purity of Galileo's motives; the children will not abandon their belief that Marina is a witch.

In this extract the children are ready to believe that Marina bewitches the coachman's horses even though their account carries the more rational explanation that the cold coming through the hole in the roof caused the horses to get sick. Andrea's comment, 'A man can't know about a thing he hasn't looked into . . .' and his challenge to the children's prejudice is directly relevant to the action of the rest of the play because Galileo challenged what appeared to be the evidence of the senses: the sun does *appear* to rise and fall. The relationship to the central theme of the play is further reinforced by the dramatic irony: the children go on with their game unaware of the significance of the book which Andrea is taking out of the country.

The incident here serves as an analogy for what happens in the play as a whole but some critics have seen the work itself as an analogy for what was happening in Brecht's Germany at the time. Two versions of the play were written and critics have seen references to contemporary concerns in both. 'In the 1930s . . . what presumably commended the subject of Galileo to Brecht was the analogy between the seventeenth-century scientists' underground activities and those of twentieth-century left-wingers in Hitler's Germany' (Bentley, 1966: 16). Brecht identified the motivating force for the new version of the play, 'The atomic age made its debut at Hiroshima in the middle of our work. Overnight the biography of the founder of the new system of physics read differently.' (ibid.: 16). To see the play as an analogy for contemporary events however is not necessarily to circumscribe its meaning; it can both parallel contemporary events and explore more general concepts. Similarly, the events of Arthur Miller's *The Crucible* have parallels with the McCarthy anti-Communist 'witch-hunt' in America, but the play is also about more universal themes to do with moral panic, personal integrity and truth.

The use of analogy in drama teaching is widely seen in the literature as a technique for distancing events which might otherwise be too sensitive to treat directly. The analysis here indicates that analogy can also be used to highlight more general themes of the drama.

Examples

The text extract itself, because it is self-contained, can provide a useful stimulus for drama work. It is short enough to be performed. The children's verse at the beginning and end of the scene gives it unity and sets an appropriate atmosphere while the set and shadow present interesting technical challenges. Without knowledge of the play overall, the scenes with the custom's officer and children seem to have little connection and for the first enactment the exchange with the custom's officer can be omitted or the participants can be asked to speculate on what the book might actually be about. Focusing on this scene could be a helpful 'way in' to the whole text.

The extract can be used as a starting point for a drama about Marina. What is the truth about her? What sort of life does she lead? What do the other neighbours think about her? Drama activities based on 'The Truth About Marina' might include:

- creation of tableaux representing scenes from her former life;
- questioning in role of neighbours to establish the extent of their knowledge and attitudes;
- an encounter between Marina and one of the children which changes the latter's mind about her;
- creation of scenes which demonstrate the way the children's prejudices are reinforced by adults;
- exploration of a scene in which the children pluck up courage to talk their way into the home;
- we hear Marina's thoughts being spoken aloud as she listens to the chant of the children in the street outside – the children's words haunt her as she goes about her daily business.

The practice of working on a parallel scene which represents the main theme which the drama seeks to explore is familiar to drama practitioners. Neelands (1990) provides two examples: a drama about the persecution of the Jews is actually presented as a play about space travellers fleeing to another planet; a play about pollution is explored through a legend about the last of the dragons imprisoned beneath the ice. O'Toole (1992) describes the exploration of the theme of racism with a group in which there were some very real tensions by setting the fictional context for the drama in seventeenth-century England. Byron (1986) describes how the experience of a narrative text can be enhanced by working not directly on the text itself in drama but on parallel scenes. This is often quite a useful way into narrative fiction. Golding's *Lord of the Flies*, for example, can be introduced by exploring analogy whereby pupils are left alone in the classroom by the teacher to 'get on with their work' – can they manage without an adult or does chaos ensue? Heathcote (see Johnson and O'Neill, 1984: 207) has drawn attention to another use of analogy as 'the best way of making something fresh and worthy of consideration when it has become too cliche-ridden, too familiar, too full of prejudice because of memory and past weariness. It provides a new face for old material.' Familiar dramas about school, teenage/parent tension, family quarrels can be given fresh impetus and humorous twists by setting the drama on planet Zarg.

The examples given by Neelands and O'Toole quite rightly emphasise the distancing effect of the use of analogy to allow the treatment of sensitive issues, while Heathcote draws attention to the pragmatic reasons for using the technique. I want to suggest that, as indicated above, analogy can also be important as a way of gaining understanding of how drama works as an art form. Analogy relies on the ability to create a scene which parallels the original focus of interest. This in turn necessitates the identification of a theme or universal which is common to both. Drama works through concrete, particular incidents, but the creation of dual situations with common elements highlights the universal themes.

The use of analogy, then, can:
- distance the events to which the drama alludes;
- invigorate well-worn themes;
- throw light on the original theme;
- draw attention to universal aspects which are being depicted.

The following drama project was ostensibly about the repression of the theatre in Puritan England. It could however provide an analogy for a specific event, e.g. the failure to include drama as a separate subject in the National Curriculum, the banning of a performance of a play in school because it is considered unsuitable. In addition, and not necessarily as an alternative, it can act as metaphor for any suppression of beliefs by an authoritarian body. The lesson sequence was as follows:

1. Teacher reads the proclamation announcing the suppression of drama. This leads to discussion which establishes some of the basic facts about Puritan England. It is important that lack of historical knowledge does not inhibit the engagement in the drama but the participation in the project can motivate participants to find out the contextual information they need.

An Ordnance of the Lords and Commons, assembled in Parliament, for the Lord Mayor of the City of London, and the Justices of the Peace, to suppress Stage-plays and Interludes, &c.

Die Veneris, Octob. 22, 1647

For the better suppression of Stage-plays, Interludes, and Common Players.
It is this day ordered, by the Lords and Commons in Parliament assembled, that the Lord Mayor, Justices of the Peace, and Sheriffs of the City of London and Westminster, the Counties of Middlesex and

Surrey, or any two or more of them, shall and may, and are hereby authorised and required to enter into all houses, and other places within the city of London, and liberties thereof, and other places within their respective jurisdictions, where stage plays, interludes, or other common plays are or shall be acted or played, and all such common Players or Actors, as they upon view of them, or any one of them, or upon oaths by two credible witnesses (which they are hereby authorised to minister), shall be proved before them, or any two of them, to have acted or played in such Playhouses or places abovesaid: and all person and persons so offending to commit to any common jail or prison, there to remain until the next general Sessions of the Peace, holden within the said City of London or Liberties thereof, and places aforesaid, or sufficient security entered for his or their appearance at the said Sessions, there to be punished as Rogues, according to law.

> *J. Brown, Cleric. Parliamentorum.*
> *Hen. Elsynge, Cler. Parl. Dom. Com.*

2. In groups of four or five, participants are asked to create a tableau showing a typical Puritan family at meal-time, at prayer. The use of tableau means that the participants do not have to be constrained by their limited factual knowledge. However the exercise can raise specific questions about the customs and behaviour at the time which can be addressed.

3. Tableaux to be repeated, but this time the still image betrays subtly that one member of the family does not share exactly the same values as the others. Extracts from the proclamation are read as the tableaux are performed.

4. The 'outsiders' from each family meet secretly to rehearse their play (see Chapter 20: Play Within A Play) while the other members of the family air their suspicions that they have a renegade in their midst. The contrast between the family gathering and the rehearsal aims to capture the contrasting texture and mood.

5. The 'outsiders' or 'actors' are challenged when they return home and have to defend their actions.

The drama explores family tensions and the repression of beliefs in the context of a specific historical period. Analogy is the specific and deliberate use of one context to parallel another but it also helps to highlight the more general theme. In this case the project culminates in an exploration of the value of drama and art.

CHAPTER THREE

Beginnings

The interior of the Prozorovs' house. OLGA *stands correcting exercise books.* MASHA *sits reading a book.* IRINA *stands lost in her own thoughts.*

OLGA: It's exactly a year since Father died. A year ago today – May the fifth – it was on your name-day, Irina. It was very cold, we had snow. I thought I should never survive it, and there you were lying in a dead faint. But now here's a year gone by, and we can think about it again quite calmly. You're back in white, your face is shining . . .

The clock strikes twelve.

The clock kept striking then, too.

Pause.

I remember the band playing as they carried Father's body on the bier. I remember them firing the volley over the grave. He was a general, he had a brigade, but not many people came. Though it was raining at the time. Sleeting – sleeting hard.

IRINA: Why keep harking back?

BARON TUSENBACH, CHEBUTYKIN, *and* SOLYONY *appear on the other side of the colonnade, around the table in the main room.*

OLGA: It's warm today. We can have the windows wide. The birch trees aren't out yet, though. Father got his brigade and left Moscow with us eleven years ago, and I well remember what Moscow was like at this time of year, at the beginning of May. Everything would be in blossom already, everything would be warm, everything would be awash with sunshine. Eleven years have gone by, but I remember it all as if it were yesterday. Oh God, I woke up this morning, I saw the light flooding in, I saw the spring, and I felt such a great surge of joy, such a passionate longing for home.

CHEBUTYKIN: Stuff and nonsense, sir!
TUSENBACH: Utter rubbish, of course.

MASHA, *lost in thought over her book, quietly whistles a tune.*

OLGA: Don't whistle, Masha. How could you?

Pause.

I'm at school each day, then I give lessons for the rest of the afternoon, and I end up with a perpetual headache, I end up thinking the kind of thoughts I'd have if I were an old woman already. And in fact these last four years since I've been teaching I have felt as if day by day, drop by drop, my youth and strength were going out of me. And the only thing that grows, the only thing that gets stronger, is one single dream . . .
IRINA: To go to Moscow. To sell up the house, to finish with everything here and off to Moscow . . .
OLGA: Yes! To Moscow, as soon as ever we can!

CHEBUTYKIN *and* TUSENBACH *laugh.*

IRINA: Our brother will most likely be a professor. All the same, he won't want to live here. The only one who's stuck here is poor Masha.
OLGA: Masha will come to Moscow for the whole summer, every year.

MASHA *quietly whistles a tune.*

Anton Chekhov, Three Sisters

Commentary

In many ways this beginning is unremarkable, chosen precisely for the fact that, in typical Chekhov style, it seems at first to lack any strong sense of dramatic potential or intensity. A certain amount of expository, factual information is given to the audience. We learn that it is Irina's nameday, it is the anniversary of the death of the sisters' father and that it is eleven years since the family left Moscow. The extract introduces the three sisters, makes mention of the brother who also lives in the house, and conveys the information that Olga is a teacher. The father had been a general and the continued presence of the army is established by the appearance of the other three characters on stage. If anything, it is the very ordinariness of what is presented that is notable.

However the extract does more than simply convey information to the audience – it also establishes a mood. The references to the weather – cold, snow, rain, sleet, warmth, sunshine – coincide with feelings of regret, nostalgia and hope. Olga's comments on her profession as a teacher create a sense of waste and decay, of time passing. The striking of the clock, the pauses, Masha's quiet whistling and the contrasting laughter of the army officers all contribute to a mood which, despite the lack of intense dramatic action, is nevertheless significant.

It would be tempting to conclude that this beginning has more lyrical than dramatic qualities, but a closer reading reveals that the dramatic quality of the extract and the subtle underlying tension derive from its treatment of the ingredient which is central to all drama – time. What we are witnessing is set in the present but there is a very strong sense of longing for the past and hope for the future. 'Everything would be in blossom already, everything would be warm, everything would be awash with sunshine' says Masha, remembering what it was like being in Moscow. The sisters look back to their childhood and forward to the future in Moscow.

One critic has suggested that at the very heart of the play is 'the sense of the difficulty that human beings have of living in the present' (Frayn, 1988: *lviii*). Williams (1952: 114) has noted an element of awkwardness and sentimentality in the type of self-revelation epitomised by Olga's speech but suggests that it is important to recognise a convention at work here. The format is that of a conversation but more is being attempted than is often realised in conversation. The lyrical mood, the sense of regret for the past and hopes for the future are key aspects of the type of beginning the author uses here and arise directly from the way he creates dialogue.

My interest in this chapter is not primarily how the necessary information is conveyed to the audience (which is addressed in Chapter 6: Exposition) but the different ways in which a play can start. Exposition is nevertheless a consideration because many plays depend on withholding information at the start. Shaffer's *Amadeus* begins with one of the main characters, Salieri, on stage near the end of his life while accusatory voices fill the auditorium. The rest of the play covers events from his earlier life (see Chapter 25: Voices). Many of Shakespeare's plays (particularly the tragedies) open with minor characters on stage talking about the main protagonist before the latter makes an entrance. The start may be deliberately intriguing and confusing, as with Stoppard's *After Magritte* which confronts the audience with a bizarre tableau, the meaning of which gradually becomes apparent as the play progresses.

Many dramatists start in the middle of a dialogue; at the start of Dario Fo's *Accidental Death of an Anarchist* the audience finds itself listening to an interrogation which is already in mid-flight. Similarly *Class Enemy* (Nigel Williams) begins in the middle of a conversation. Action rather than dialogue may engage the audience's attention as, for example, at the start of Trevor Griffiths' *The Comedians* when we watch the caretaker of the school erasing graffiti from the blackboard; the use of song or direct address to the audience (Jorn Arden's *The Waters of Babylon*) are other examples of ways in which writers begin their works. All need to take account of the time element which contributes to the structure of the play – events from the past have invariably determined the dramatic present.

Studying how dramatists construct beginnings provides a valuable insight into the art of the playwright but can also inform teachers' and pupils' approaches to their improvised drama. The example from Chekhov highlights the way the beginning can set a mood and establish central themes as well as communicate expository information.

Examples

Many drama books contain interesting ideas for starting points for drama such as newspaper articles, poems, objects, letters, maps, games and so on. My focus in this section is not so much the stimulus for the drama but on how the dramatic action itself is initiated. I propose to consider two common ways in which teachers initiate drama with pupils and the lessons which can be learned from considering the ways in which dramatists work. I will then discuss the ways in which pupils can be helped to find methods of initiating their own small-group work.

Teacher in role

'Teacher in role' is an extremely valuable technique which is particularly appropriate for younger pupils because it can make the drama more real, deepen the work, provide challenges to pupils' thinking and set an appropriate tone. Readman and Lamont (1994) provide descriptions of lessons initiated by using this technique with the teacher variously taking the part of a mother with her two ill children (pre-school), a child who is frightened to go to a new school (five to six year olds), and a newspaper reporter (seven to nine year olds). In each case the drama needs a minimal amount of pre-structuring with the children because they are immediately drawn into the fiction. Bolton (1992) describes examples of different lessons in which he as teacher adopted the roles of a stranger bringing news of Robin Hood's activities, a hospital doctor and a zoo keeper. The possibilities are endless and the power of the technique widely acknowledged in the drama literature. Other accounts of 'teacher in role' are given in Heathcote (see Johnson and O'Neill, 1984), and Morgan and Saxton (1987).

Despite its effectiveness as a way of initiating drama, many teachers, having been faced by pupils who fail to take the teacher's efforts seriously, will attest to the fact that the technique is not without its risks. Problems sometimes occur because pupils fail to read the signs appropriately or the signing has not been sufficiently clear. At the start of a play the audience have what Esslin has described as 'key signs' which determine the overall reading. Aspects such as the style of the language, the mood created by the set and the performance, the description of the genre of the play (whether, for example, it is billed as a comedy or tragedy) all help the audience key into the appropriate response. If pupils are confronted too suddenly by 'teacher in role' they respond in ways which to the teacher are inappropriate. The convention may require gradual introduction rather than sudden imposition by, for example:

- acting out a series of actions;
- a conversation on the telephone for pupils to discuss before seeking to engage them in the drama;
- asking the pupils themselves to help create the role, e.g. How would he speak? How should he behave?
- establishing the context with the pupils before initiating the role, e.g. Where is the scene taking place? What is the likely reaction to this person?

Use of tableaux

Use of tableaux is also a technique which has been widely discussed in recent writing on drama. It has a pragmatic value as a convention because it culminates in quiet, concentrated work, has enormous potential for depth and is fairly easily managed by most pupils. Its value as a way of beginning drama derives from the fact that it avoids the onward rush of narrative which can work against the quality of work. It was suggested earlier that all dramatists in some way have to take account of the past in their creation of the dramatic present. The creation of a tableau is the ultimate slowing down of the action because it isolates and freezes a moment in time and necessarily takes account of what has happened before. The right sort of tableau can help pupils gain entry into a dramatic plot. If we take the most action-driven topics which pupils might want to choose as the focus of their drama, such as a bank robbery, and create the right kind of tableau, the beginnings of an unfolding dramatic plot appear. The task to 'create the exact moment when one of the gang made up his mind that he would have to betray his colleagues' is a very different task from asking pupils to 'create a still image of a bank robbery'.

When writing narrative fiction, young children have at their disposal the convention of 'Once upon a time' which, although clichéd, provides them with a way of getting started. Even if they do not use those actual words, they are familiar with similar narrative conventions, such as 'There once was a small boy who . . .'. There is no similar convention in drama and it is not uncommon for pupils of any age in their small-group work not to know how to begin. This problem may not arise if the teacher is highly directive, but part of pupils' acquisition of dramatic skill is to be able to create and sustain drama themselves.

The following examples are some of the ways in which the teacher can support them by providing suggestions which may initiate the work. Let us imagine that the focus of the drama is on the plight of the elderly in society and moral responsibilities. A decision about what to do about an elderly relative is causing a rift in the family, some members of which think he/she is no longer able to live at home.

• Supply the first two lines of dialogue;

This simple solution can be very effective. It can help identify tone, context, central theme.

'I called into the Rookstone home today – they have a vacancy.'
'Rookstone – but that's miles away.'

The dialogue signals to the participants that the difference of opinion may not be expressed directly by the participants. Initially, there is a constraint on the row which may develop.

• Suggest a set of framing actions;

Here the group is given a set of actions to perform before the dialogue begins which helps to frame the dialogue which ensues. One character helps the elderly relative move very, very slowly from one chair to another before the conversation begins about him/her in hushed tones. Alternatively, at the start of the scene, one member of the family is clearing up a plate of food which was dropped by the elderly relative who is no longer in the room.

• Introduce a character entrance;

The drama begins with the entrance of one of the family who assumes, wrongly, that a decision has already been made.

• Use music to establish mood;

This can be incorporated into the actual scene or simply used to fade into the action. Here the intention is to help pupils establish atmosphere rather than meaning, but one may well follow readily after the other.

29

- Direct address to audience;

    Here one or more of the characters address the audience directly before the start of the drama. It could be the elderly relative who is only given a real identity in the monologue at the start.
- Avoiding the subject;

    The group are told that the first six or so lines of dialogue should not address what is on everyone's mind but the tension is apparent.
- Voices;

    As the old person sits alone, voices from the past fill the room. There is a pause before the other family members enter and the more naturalistic drama begins.

The Chekhov example is particularly interesting because it contrasts with emphasis on plot and action which often preoccupies pupils in their drama. By focusing very deliberately on beginnings, the emphasis on 'What will happen next?' is likely to give way to other more subtle means of creating tension.

CHAPTER FOUR

Counterpoint

The scene is in a pub where Fluther Good and the young lad Covey have been engaged in a drunken argument partly focused on Rosie.

(FLUTHER *suddenly springs into the middle, flings his hat into the corner, whips off his coat, and begins to paw the air.*)

FLUTHER (*roaring at the top of his voice*): Come on, come on, you lowser; put your mits up now, if there's a man's blood in you! Be God, in a few minutes you'll see some snots flyin' around, I'm tellin' you . . . When Fluther's done with you, you'll have a vice versa opinion of him! Come on, now, come on!

BARMAN (*running from behind the counter and catching hold of the* COVEY): Here, out you go, me little bowsey. Because you got a couple o' halves you think you can act as you like. (*He pushes the* COVEY *to the door*) Fluther's a friend o' mine, an' I'll not have him insulted.

THE COVEY (*struggling with the* BARMAN): Ay, leggo, leggo there; fair hunt, give a man a fair hunt! One minute with him is all I ask; one minute alone with him, while you're runnin' for th' priest an' th' doctor.

FLUTHER (*to the* BARMAN): Let him go, let him go, Tom! let him open th' door to sudden death if he wants to!

BARMAN (*to the* COVEY): Go on, out you go an' do th' bowsey somewhere else. (*He pushes the* COVEY *out and comes back.*)

ROSIE (*getting* FLUTHER's *hat as he is putting on his coat*): Be God, you put th' fear o' God in his heart that time! I thought you'd have to be dug out of him . . . . Th' way you lepped out without any of your fancy side-steppin'! 'Men like Fluther,' say I to meself, 'is gettin' scarce nowadays.'

FLUTHER (*with proud complacency*): I wasn't goin' to let meself be malignified by a chancer . . . . He got a little bit too derogatory for Fluther . . . . Be God, to think of a cur like that comin' to talk to a man like me!

ROSIE (*fixing on his hat*): Did j'ever!

FLUTHER: He's lucky he got off safe. I hit a man last week, Rosie, an' he's fallin' yet!

ROSIE: Sure, you'd ha' broken him in two if you'd ha' hitten him one clatther!

FLUTHER (*amorously, putting his arm around* ROSIE): Come on into th' snug, me little darlin', an' we'll have a few dhrinks before I see you home.

ROSIE: Oh, Fluther, I'm afraid you're a terrible man for th' women.

(*They go into the snug as* CLITHEROE, CAPTAIN BRENNAN and LIEUT. LANGON *of the Irish volunteers enter hurriedly.* CAPTAIN BRENNAN *carries the banner of The Plough and the Stars, and* LIEUT. LANGON *a green, white, and orange Tri-colour. They are in a state of emotional excitement. Their faces are flushed and their eyes sparkle; they speak rapidly, as if unaware of the meaning of what they said. They have been mesmerised by the fervency of the speeches.*)

CLITHEROE (*almost pantingly*): Three glasses o' port!

(*The* BARMAN *brings the drinks.*)

CAPT. BRENNAN: We won't have long to wait now.

LIEUT. LANGON: Th' time is rotten ripe for revolution.

CLITHEROE: You have a mother, Langon.

LIEUT. LANGON: Ireland is greater than a mother.

CAPT. BRENNAN: You have a wife, Clitheroe.

CLITHEROE: Ireland is greater than a wife.

LIEUT. LANGON: Th' time for Ireland's battle is now – th' place for Ireland's battle is here.

Sean O'Casey, The Plough and the Stars

Commentary

The events of this scene from Act Two take place in Dublin in Easter 1916 just before the uprising against British rule. O'Casey deliberately sets the petty squabble in the pub alongside the rhetoric of the members of the Irish volunteers. One effect of putting the two scenes side by side is to contrast them; the complacency and lack of awareness of Fluther and Rosie (Covey, although naive, is more political in the play) could be compared with the commitment and single-mindedness of the volunteers. However, in the wider context of the play as a whole it is apparent that the audience may be being invited to draw *parallels and comparisons*, not just *contrasts* between the two scenes. What could be judged as the empty rhetoric and false heroism of the Irish volunteers may well have more in common with the comic posturing of Fluther than is first apparent. Both have an exaggerated sense of their own power and possibilities, both believe they are acting from principles. I have coined the term 'counterpoint' (rather than contrast) to refer to any deliberate juxtaposition of scenes in drama in a way which adds to the meaning and throws light on both. Contrast, comparison and repetition all come within this category.

The three Irish volunteers who enter the pub at the end of this extract have been listening to a speech at a republican rally. The entire scene takes place in the pub but extracts of the speech are heard at various points throughout, providing with its heightened rhetoric another contrast with the squabbles and fights within. In this extract the style and tone of the language of the volunteers, with its ritualistic incantation bordering on melodrama, is contrasted with that of Fluther with his colloquialisms and comic malapropisms.

It would be wrong to oversimplify the author's intent. The scene which brought the flag of the Irish Republic into the pub and which showed a prostitute on stage while an actual republican speech was being delivered caused riots at the Abbey Theatre in Dublin when the play was shown. The play does not glorify the heroes of the republican movement, nor does it seek to deny their courage and commitment; in later scenes it mocks the characters whose first act after the uprising is to loot the shops, but it also demonstrates their humanity and mutual loyalty. The ironic contrasts and humour defy any simplistic analysis. The effect of placing two scenes side by side is to convey meanings which are not necessarily very precisely defined. They provoke thought rather than confine thinking – what is significant is that each scene gains more meaning by being contrasted with the other. At the very end of the scene from which this extract is taken Rosie sings a song, 'I once had a lover', which recounts a sexual adventure with a sailor and the birth of 'a bright bouncin' boy' just as the Irish volunteers march off to battle and, for many of them, certain death. The effect is aesthetic and thought-provoking rather than discursive and didactic. The effect of counterpoint is to render the meaning more complex because it derives as much from the juxtaposition of two scenes as from explicit statements contained in one or other.

States (1994) uses the term 'counterpoint' to describe a rather more specific and specialised technique whereby two separate dialogues ironically overlap. He uses an example from Chekhov's *Three Sisters* (see Chapter 3).

> OLGA: . . . Oh God, I woke up this morning, I saw the light flooding in, I saw the spring, and I felt such a great surge of joy, such a passionate longing for home.
> CHEBUTYKIN: Stuff and nonsense, sir!
> TUSENBACH: Utter rubbish, of course.

The conversation being held by Chebutykin and Tusenbach is completely separate and not intended as a response to Olga's words but, by setting them against each other in this way, the creation of a subtext is possible which draws attention to the 'indifference of a world running in counter rhythm to human longings' (States, 1994: 98). While this type of weaving together of two dialogues is technically demanding, it illustrates the way in which the combination of two pieces of script can introduce new meanings. An example is given below of how monologues can be effectively combined.

Examples

There is a degree of overlap between the use of 'counterpoint' and 'alternative perspectives' described in Chapter 1 as both use common methods. However alternative perspective tends to focus on one scene (providing alternative versions, or contrasting thoughts, letters, diaries), whereas with counterpoint the focus is on two different scenes. Similarly, instead of letters, reports, diaries casting a different perspective on the scene which is enacted, the written documents are not necessarily *directly* related to the focus of the drama. Counterpoint can be employed by teachers in order to structure a set of drama activities or by pupils themselves as a way of giving depth and form to their own small-group play making.

A very simple example will illustrate the possibilities for structuring drama which become available when the technique is employed. Take the case of a realistic social drama – a teenager has been invited to go on holiday with friends for the first time and has not yet told her parents. Given the task of creating a polished improvisation based on this idea, pupils instinctively might work through two scenes chronologically: for example, the invitation which occurs in the course of a conversation with a friend, followed by a confrontation with parents. Using counterpoint technique, the first scene can be followed by or interwoven with a scene (which in real time may be happening simultaneously) in which the parents' plans for the family holiday are also being discussed. Rather than focus on simple conflict, the contrasting scenes explore with potential poignancy the perspective and disappointment of the parents. The intention is not to moralise but to reveal complexities, as in O'Casey's play.

The following examples of counterpoint provide ready-made content for drama:

- the reading of a school report describing a pupil as being highly immature and childish is set against a scene showing the degree of responsibility for a younger sibling assumed by the same pupil at home;
- a tableau which shows an act of bullying is set against another tableau in which the victim in the first version is one of the perpetrators in the second;
- a scene which shows the positive aspects of living in the city is set against one which shows the disadvantages;
- a dialogue between nurse and old person in a home is set against the family of the latter deciding to cancel their visit that particular week;
- a radio announcement about chemical waste from a factory polluting a river is set against a board meeting in the factory in which the directors are planning an expansion to the business after a profitable year.

In each of these cases the juxtaposition of two aspects of the theme suggests a further meaning but does not circumscribe it – the drama works obliquely. The same technique can be used as a starting point for group work which has a more focused curriculum objective. As part of a project on religions of the world, an RE textbook instructs pupils to 'Make up a short play about someone who acts with the wrong motivation'. Set in that way, the task is demanding because unless it is constructed with some subtlety the result is likely to be fairly crude. For example, scene one might show a neighbour calling on an elderly woman to offer to do the shopping, and in scene two the same man is discussing with his wife whether, as a result of his kindness, she is likely to include him in her will.

An alternative way of setting the task is to ask the pupils to show two scenes depicting (a) a situation in which an individual engages in some act of kindness (e.g. a businessman is visited by a charity worker who asks for a donation) and (b) a situation in which the same person receives some reward as a direct result of the action (e.g. the businessman receives news that he has been awarded a knighthood). The juxtaposition of the two scenes does not at first impute any simple false motive. The pupils could be asked to repeat the two scenes in such a way that there is a hint that the original motives were not pure.

Another approach might be to provide a thank-you letter as stimulus for the drama. The letter, as well as being an aesthetic counterpoint in the enactment, also acts as a method of exposition and contextualisation, freeing the pupils to concentrate on the question of the character's intentions. Again, the task for the pupils now is to show through the drama how the motive *may have been* less than pure. The emphasis on the uncertainty and ambiguity of the motivation is an essential element of both the success of the drama and the learning about human behaviour.

1. The letter is read to the class:

Dear John,

I just wanted to drop you a note to thank you for your great kindness the other day. I am sorry I was a bit suspicious when you called but you have to be so careful these days. The hedge and front garden look lovely now after all your hard work. I have written to Sam to thank him as well.

I hope your project goes well at school and perhaps you might call around again some day.

Best wishes,

Mrs May Bell

2. Discussion: What is the context? Who are the characters? What is the project to which Mrs Bell refers? Does it have anything to do with the boys' visit?

3. Small-group drama which sheds light on the pupils' motivation – e.g. the scene which took place prior to the boys knocking on the door; a scene which shows what prompted the idea (they may be collecting points towards winning a prize in school or gaining some proficiency badge).

4. Discussion of the boys' motivation and whether their motives could be described as pure. Does it matter that their act of kindness brought them some benefit?

5. Scenes to be developed to show further insight into the motivation and presented in conjunction with a reading of the letter.

Simner (1994) describes an interesting example of using a technique in script writing which could come under the general heading of 'counterpoint': combining different monologues. The participants have to think of a situation in which two people meet after a long period of separation, e.g. an adopted child meeting the natural parent or a husband visiting his wife in prison. The short monologues are written according to a specific structure, e.g. the journey, the meeting, the return, the epilogue which sums up the event. Tension is included by specifying that one of the characters is looking forward to the meeting, the other is dreading it. The key development then is for the two characters to dovetail the monologues sentence by sentence so that the thoughts start to interact in the manner of a dialogue. This is a challenging task suitable for older pupils.

The task is a valuable activity in itself but it could also be usefully incorporated into a more extended drama project because it allows potentially difficult emotional scenes to be handled effectively. The use of the technique provides distance and obliquity without denying the strength of the emotional engagement.

CHAPTER FIVE

Endings

MARY: There's his prologue.
RALPH: The prologue. I forgot.

Pause

Let me hear it.
WISEHAMMER: From distant climes o'er wide-spread seas we come,
Though not with much éclat or beat of drum,
True patriots all; for be it understood,
We left our country for our country's good;
No private views disgraced our generous zeal,
What urg'd our travels was our country's weal,
And none will doubt but that our emigration
Has prov'd most useful to the British nation.

Silence

RALPH: When Major Ross hears that, he'll have an apoplectic fit.
MARY: I think it's very good.
DABBY: So do I. And true.
SIDEWAY: It's very good, Wisehammer, it's very well written, but it's too –
too political. It will be considered provocative.
WISEHAMMER: You don't want me to say it.
RALPH: Not tonight. We have many people against us.
WISEHAMMER: I could tone it down. I could omit 'We left our country for
our country's good.'
DABBY: That's the best line.
RALPH: It would be wrong to cut it.
WISEHAMMER: I worked so hard on it.
LIZ: It rhymes.
SIDEWAY: We'll use it in the Sideway Theatre.

RALPH: You will get much praise as Brazen, Wisehammer.

WISEHAMMER: It isn't the same as writing.

RALPH: The theatre is like a small republic, it requires private sacrifices for the good of the whole. That is something you should agree with, Wisehammer.

Pause

And now, my actors, I want to say what a pleasure it has been to work with you. You are on your own tonight and you must do your utmost to provide the large audience out there with a pleasurable, intelligible and memorable evening.

LIZ: We will do our best, Mr Clark.

MARY: I love this!

RALPH: Arscott.

ARSCOTT (*to* CAESAR): You walk three steps ahead of me. If you stumble once, you know what will happen to you later? Move!

RALPH: You're on.

ARSCOTT *is about to go on, then remembers.*

ARSCOTT: Halberd! Halberd!

He is handed his halberd and goes up stage and off, preceded by CAESAR *beating the drum. Backstage, the remaining actors listen with trepidation to* KITE's *first speech.*

'If any gentlemen soldiers, or others, have a mind to serve Her Majesty, and pull down the French King; if any prentices have severe masters, any children have undutiful parents; if any servants have too little wages or any husband too much wife; let them repair to the noble Sergeant Kite, at the Sign of the Raven, in this good town of Shrewsbury, and they shall receive present relief and entertainment' . . .

And to the triumphant music of Beethoven's Fifth Symphony and the sound of applause and laughter from the First Fleet audience, the first Australian performance of The Recruiting Officer *begins.*

Timberlake Wertenbaker, *Our Country's Good*

Commentary

The play ends just as another play, Farquhar's *The Recruiting Officer*, is about to be performed. The fact that the actors who are about to 'perform' are convicts who have been transported to Australia from England in 1788 means that the success in getting the play on stage is a considerable achievement. The performance of *The Recruiting Officer* and the overcoming of various obstacles which might have prevented its realisation constitute the central structural thrust of Wertenbaker's play. The barbaric conditions, the opposition of other officers, the squabblings and initial shortcomings of the convicts, along with accusations of wrong-doing against them, conspire to make the success of the project seem unlikely. It is therefore not necessary for any of the performance itself or its aftermath to be shown because the important thing is the fulfilment of the ambition. Thus the ending of *Our Country's Good* encapsulates one of the central features of drama – it is the overcoming of the constraints which work against the fulfilment of the goal which is the source of the tension and which constitutes the drama, rather than any need to dwell on the realisation of the goal itself.

It is fitting therefore that the play should end at the point when the other performance, the 'play within a play', begins. It is a partial resolution but it also looks to the short- and long-term future. As will be discussed below, modern drama tends to employ more 'open' than 'closed' endings. Nevertheless, to end with a beginning, so to speak, might run the risk of leaving an unsatisfied feeling. Endings have an aesthetic function irrespective of their structural significance. It is worth noticing, therefore, the features in this extract which give a sense of resolution: the prologue written by one of the convicts gives voice for the first time to the title of Wertenbaker's play; the rhyming couplets (used in Shakespearean drama to mark endings) contribute to the feeling of an impending end; the brief summary and reminder of what the actors have been working against – 'We have many people against us' – and Ralph's short speech add to the feeling of finality and resolution. Whether or not an ending serves to resolve the plot as in more classical drama, the drama needs to have a sense of convergence, a feeling that this is where events were leading us to be aesthetically satisfying. This is equally true of modern drama which experiments with inconclusive or ambiguous endings. Unusual endings have to emerge from the internal logic of the play and relate to what has come before in order to be successful.

Wertenbaker's play celebrates the power and value of theatre. The author describes her intention to explore 'the redemptive power of the theatre, of art for people who have been silenced.' It is therefore appropriate symbolically that the play should end with the triumph of the performance of *The Recruiting Officer* towards which they have been striving. Structural, contextual and aesthetic considerations inform the dramatist's choice of ending.

Barthes' distinction between the '*plaisir*' of the classic, comfortable text corresponding with closed endings and the '*jouissance*' of the unsettling, radical text is helpful here because it is a reminder that, if participants have preconceptions of certain types of ending, they are likely to be bewildered if those are not fulfilled. Classical theorists, whether evoking concepts such as 'resolution', 'denouement' or 'catastrophe', shared a common view of the dramatic ending as being the resolution of questions and conflicts and the abolition of any discrepancies in the audience's understanding (Pfister 1988: 95). Conflicts are resolved, as are moral ambiguities. Open endings, as the label suggests, do not provide such a resolution and are more characteristic of modern drama. The structuring of drama within a temporal framework which coincides with performance time (i.e. the time which the play actually takes, as opposed to the time which the narrative would demand) helps to provide the audience with a 'sense of an ending' (Aston and Savona, 1991). However, a sense of an ending is not reliant purely on the dramatic structure, and may rely on other factors such as the use of language, action, lighting, music. Recognition of this fact can be very helpful for teachers and pupils when creating drama.

Examples of more classical conventional endings can be found in Shakespeare's plays which may conclude the plot but do not necessarily bring an end to the narrative – the ending may in fact point towards the future. In both the tragedies and comedies there is a sense of the restoration of order and frequently the sense of a new beginning. At the end of *Romeo and Juliet* the plot is disclosed for the first time to the characters on stage and final comment is made in verse on the lovers' death. The use of rhyme contributes to the sense of closure.

> For never was a story of more woe
> Than this of Juliet and her Romeo.

King Lear ends with the restoration of order and comment on the tragedy. Here there is no strong sense of a future: the weight of the verse is on the present and what has just been witnessed.

> Speak what we feel, not what we ought to say.
> The oldest hath borne most; we that are young
> Shall never see so much nor live so long.

Dance and festivities come at the end of *Much Ado About Nothing* but there is also a tidying up of the action so that no part of the plot is left unresolved; we learn that the Prince's brother will be punished in due course. Again, the implication is that the narrative will carry on after the end of the play but this does not detract from the sense of final resolution.

> Think not on him till to-morrow; I'll devise thee brave punishments for him. Strike up pipers.

In contrast to *Much Ado About Nothing, A Midsummer Night's Dream* concludes with an epilogue by Puck which has a metatheatrical function, drawing attention to the play as fiction. Ironically, Puck's words have a parallel with the concerns of the mechanicals in the 'play within a play' (Chapter 20) not to offend the audience.

> If we shadows have offended,
> Think but this and all is mended
> That you have but slumb'red here
> While these visions did appear.

Twelfth Night ends with a song in which Feste also draws attention to the theatricality of the play.

> But that's all one, our play is done,
> And we'll strive to please you every day.

These classical endings can be contrasted with more unusual endings of the modern theatre. The endings of both Ionesco's *Bald Prima Donna* and Becket's *Waiting for Godot* echo the beginnings of the play; the cyclical process, contravening the convention of the well-made play, conveys the sense of a lasting condition to which the characters are condemned. Ayckbourn's *Sisterly Feelings* has alternative endings on which the audience make a choice. Wilde's *Lady Windermere's Fan* has an interesting ending both for a comedy and for its time because the author avoids the type of 'collective disclosure' one would normally associate with the genre (Ellman, 1987: 344). Three secrets are left at the end undisclosed to the characters on stage: Windermere will never know that his wife was on the verge of running away with someone else; Lady Windermere will never know who her real mother was; Lord Augustus will never know that he has been fooled. Deception, which is one of the play's central themes, is left as a strong impression at the end.

Examples

This section will describe some examples of endings which teachers and pupils can employ in their own play making, but there is a general lesson which can be learned from the work of dramatists. Whether the drama takes a classical form, which seeks to transform a narrative into a dramatic plot culminating in a resolution of tensions, or whether it takes a more radical approach, I would maintain that a sense of ending is important. As seen in the examples, this can derive from aesthetic aspects of the drama which are not strictly structural – the type of language and the use of techniques such as ritual and song can provide the appropriate end. Plays like *Waiting for Godot* which flout the conventions of the well-made play nevertheless have an appropriate sense of ending brought about by the unity of the return to a beginning.

The other distinction which needs to be made (as in the case of the discussion of beginnings in Chapter 3) is between the teacher ending drama projects and the kinds of considerations pupils need to bear in mind when engaged in small-group play making. In *Starting Drama Teaching* I listed a number of factors which distinguish drama from dramatic play. One of these has to do with endings. Drama has a structure which works towards fulfilment. In contrast, in dramatic playing there is a 'to-and-fro' movement which is not tied to any goal which would bring the activity to an end.

The practice of getting pupils into groups to present a play can easily go awry because of the preoccupation with narrative which they find difficult to translate into plot. Pupils are therefore often uncertain about how to bring their work to an end. They need to be taught how to do this as a drama skill rather than be given the simple injunction to 'make sure it has an ending.'

Examples of endings

- alternative endings;

   The use of alternative endings is quite difficult to build into the structure of the drama but can help crystallise the dilemma at the centre of the work. A play which explores the problems of the old in society and which has focused on the problems faced by an extended family shows two endings providing possible courses of action; one in which the old person leaves for a home, the other in which he or she remains with the family.

- ambiguous endings;

   As discussed above the concept of the well-made play can dominate pupils' thinking unless they are encouraged explicitly to think about alternatives. An ambiguous ending should be deliberate and constructed. A number of dramas based on the Pied Piper recommend exploring what happens to the children when they have gone through the mountainside – partly in a desire to follow the narrative. The drama might have more impact by leaving this uncertain, as in the poem.

• use of tableaux;

In a drama sequence about a car accident which leaves the teenage victim in a persistent vegetative state, the final task for the participants is to create two family photographs before and after the incident (Bolton, 1992: 88). This activity came after a fairly intensive and emotionally demanding lesson, allowing the class to conclude and summarise the work.

• ritual;

In a drama about a mining disaster the children stand in a circle around an imaginary grave and one at a time they come forward in role as the friends of the dead miner to place flowers on his grave, speaking their thoughts as they do so (Kitson and Spiby, 1995: 39). The ending is controlled and emotionally constrained by the use of ritual.

• stage action;

The use of actions to provide an ending need not be confined to ritual. A play about a teenager leaving home can end with a simple sequence in which the character slowly packs a bag and leaves the house.

• use of song;

Bolton (1992: 81) describes a lesson with a group of six/seven year olds about the Nativity which develops in such a way that the singing of *Silent Night* at the end seems exactly appropriate. The dramatic pivot of the lesson is the sequence in which the children, by demonstrating their expertise with babies, have to persuade the teacher in role to allow the strangers to stay the night. The overcoming of this constraint provides the necessary emotional engagement for the narrative and ritualistic ending. The lesson is described more fully in the Introduction.

• use of lights;

Lights are a central aspect of the communication system in the theatre and can provide a useful way of emphasising the closure of a drama sequence. A slowly fading light can be a useful external means of establishing a particular mood, particularly if accompanied by music.

• use of reading;

This is another technique which gives a sense of aesthetic unity. Work based on poetry, a letter, will or other document which is central to the drama can be read at the end.

CHAPTER SIX

Exposition

MISS TESMAN: (*Quietly*) My goodness, they must still be in bed.

BERTE: (*Also quietly*) That's what I was telling you, miss. You know how late the steamer got in last night. And then there was all that unpacking the young lady wanted done before she would go to bed, I don't know.

MISS TESMAN: Oh, well, let them have a good sleep. But they'll be glad of some nice fresh air when they do get up. (*She goes over to the glass door and throws it wide open.*)

BERTE: (*By the table, not knowing where to put the flowers.*) There doesn't seem to be any room anywhere. I think I'll just leave them over here, miss. (*She puts the flowers by the piano.*)

MISS TESMAN: Well, Berte dear, you've got a new mistress now. God knows, parting with you was almost more than I could bear.

BERTE: (*Close to tears*) What do you think it's like for me, miss? It's years and years I've been working for you.

MISS TESMAN: We'll have to make the best of it, Berte. There's nothing else we can do. George depends on you, you see: completely. After all, you have looked after him since he was a little boy.

BERTE: Yes, but I can't stop thinking about Miss Rina, miss. Lying at home there, absolutely helpless, poor thing. And that new maid. She'll never learn how to look after an invalid properly, never.

MISS TESMAN: Oh, it won't take me long to teach her. Anyway, I shall see to most of the work myself, you know that. You needn't worry about my poor sister, Berte dear.

BERTE: But that's not the only thing, miss. I'm so frightened Mrs Tesman will think I'm not suitable.

MISS TESMAN: Oh, well, there might be one or two things when you first start . . .

BERTE: She does seem a bit superior.

MISS TESMAN: Well, that's only to be expected. She is General Gabler's daughter. Think what sort of a life she must have had when the General was alive. Do you remember how she used to go out riding with her father? That long, black riding outfit? And the feather in her hat?

BERTE: Yes, oh yes, I do. But I never thought then she would finish up marrying our little student.

MISS TESMAN: No, I didn't either. Not that George is a student any more, Berte. From now on, you'll have to call him Dr. Tesman.

BERTE: So Mrs Tesman was saying last night, soon as they set foot in the house. Is that really true, miss?

MISS TESMAN: Certainly. It's wonderful, isn't it, Berte? They made him a doctor when he was abroad, you know, on his tour. First thing I heard about it was when he told me last night on the quay.

BERTE: Well, I don't know, I'm sure he's clever enough to do anything. But I never thought he'd take up medicine.

MISS TESMAN: No, no, no, he's not that kind of doctor. (*Nods meaningfully.*) You might have to call him something even more important soon.

BERTE: And what might that be, miss?

MISS TESMAN: (*Smiling*) Aha, wouldn't you like to know? (*Moved.*) Oh, dear, oh, dear, if only poor Jochum could come back from the dead and see what's happened to his little boy. (*Looks around.*) Just a minute, Berte, what have you done? Why have you taken the loose covers off the furniture?

BERTE: Mrs Tesman said. She said she can't stand loose covers on the chairs.

MISS TESMAN: They're not going to use this room for everyday, are they?

BERTE: Yes, I think so. That's what Mrs Tesman said, anyway. He, er, the doctor, I mean, didn't open his mouth.

Henrik Ibsen, *Hedda Gabler*

Commentary

The opening exchange of *Hedda Gabler* provides the audience with a great deal of factual material. If we were to list all the details which are conveyed to the audience in this extract it would be a case of virtually repeating the whole text because each utterance is dense with significant background information. Amongst other details, it is established that Hedda Gabler has married Mr Tesman, that they have recently moved into the house, that he has just finished his studies and gained his doctorate. We also learn something of the new domestic arrangements, that the maid who has worked for Miss Tesman (who is George's aunt) will now serve Hedda and so on.

Despite the density of the factual information, it is conveyed without being laboured because it is integrated with thematic aspects of the play. These are hinted at and eventually will have greater significance. We get some inkling of Hedda's assertiveness ('there was all that unpacking the young lady wanted done before she would go to bed') and George's dependency and weakness ('George depends on you, you see: completely'). The nature of the relationship between Hedda and George is hinted at in the description of her reaction to the chair covers ('She said she can't stand loose covers on the chairs . . . He, er, the doctor, I mean, didn't open his mouth.') Aspects of the extract which seem at first to be trivial take on more significance as the play develops; moments later when Hedda enters she will refer to 'all these wretched flowers' which have so carefully been arranged.

Miss Tesman describes Hedda in a way which also takes on far more significance later in the play, 'She is General Gabler's daughter. Think what sort of a life she must have had when the General was alive. Do you remember how she used to go out riding with her father? That long, black riding outfit? And the feather in her hat?' The image captures her independence and free spirit in her former life. The significance of calling Hedda by her maiden name in the title of the play indicates that she is to be regarded as her father's daughter rather than as her husband's wife – a key insight into the reasons for the plot unfolding as it does.

Exposition continues throughout this scene, particularly in the conversation between Mrs Elvsted and Hedda in which a large number of Hedda's utterances consist entirely of questions, 'Soul mates were you? . . . Don't you trust him any more than that? . . . Who? . . . What has he told you about her? And what did he say?' This illustrates one expository technique whereby one of the characters has the same need to know as the audience.

Exposition is sometimes simply the process of conveying background information to the audience, but, as the first scene of Hedda Gabler illustrates, it can be used more subtly as a process of establishing dramatic themes and tensions. The challenge for the dramatist is not just *how* the information should be conveyed to the audience (which is how exposition is traditionally described) but selecting *how much* information is appropriate. Exposition is central to the whole dramatic structure.

The beginning of the play within a play in *The Real Inspector Hound* by Stoppard is frequently quoted as a satire on badly handled exposition because the information is conveyed so crudely. That much is true, but the humour and satire derive not just from the crass way the information is delivered but from the sense that there is in the process no withholding of information. The charwoman answers the phone as follows, 'Hello, the drawing room of Lady Muldoon's residence one morning in early spring?' She continues in conversation with one of the characters, 'Judging by the time (*she glances at the clock*) you did well to get here before high water cut us off for all practical purposes from the outside world . . . many visitors have remarked on the topographical quirk in the local strata whereby there are no roads leading from the Manor, though there *are* ways of getting *to* it, weather allowing.' The technique of exposition (despite the connotations of the phrase) is as much about withholding as it is about disclosing information.

The extent to which background information is needed varies from play to play (compare, for example, a Pinter play or *Waiting for Godot* with *King Lear* in which the initial exposition takes place in the exchange between Gloucester and Kent). Sometimes no great amount of background information is required – perhaps merely a statement of the play's central theme. Willy Russell's *Stags and Hens* announces the focus of the play from the first line as one of the characters enters the toilet singing, 'She's getting married in the morning', while his *Educating Rita* uses the technique of a telephone call. Brian Clark's *Whose Life is It Anyway?* uses banter with the nurses to establish what the audience needs to know about the illness of the central character. It is not until much later, towards the end of the play, that we hear the cause of his injuries.

Examples

Whereas drama teachers and pupils always have to address the question of how to begin drama (see Chapter 3), the concept of exposition often seems more relevant to the concerns of the dramatist than of participants in the creation of classroom drama. The reason is that very often the necessary context is defined from outside rather than from within the drama. This is true in the case of simple pairs exercises when the teacher defines for the pupils who they are, what the context is and so on. But it is also the case in more extended work when small-group plays are related to an overall project; the context and characters are usually narrowly defined so that when the work is shared the performers do not have to think about communicating necessary information.

O'Neill (1995: 45) has rightly drawn attention to the parallels between the task facing the dramatist and the leader of process drama in that both have 'to alter at a stroke our customary orientation to both time and space and locate us firmly in an alternative world, the dramatic elsewhere'. Sometimes the teacher in role will initiate a drama and the group negotiate the meaning as the work unfolds. In those cases the process of exposition is more obviously relevant. However, observation of pupils engaged in performing small-group drama work often reveals a concern to specify the context, even when the observers know what the broad situation is. This is sometimes done rather crudely as a form of prologue, 'She's the mother, he's the next door neighbour and it is nearly time for the children to come from school.' Even when there is no intention of performing to an audience, the sense of spectator in the participants often inclines them to create appropriate beginnings which define the context. Pupils who are more skilled in drama can incorporate more sophisticated expository techniques into their work.

Hornbrook (1991: 72) has argued that the 'plays in small groups' approach 'may have greater potential than its detractors admit'. What he means here is not the small-group preparation and sharing of work which is part of process drama, but work which is more free-standing and orientated to product and audience. Hornbrook has a valid argument; in a balanced drama curriculum, plays in small groups of the kind he has in mind will allow pupils to extend their *explicit* understanding of conventions like exposition, considering both *what* and *how* information needs to be conveyed. Small-group work of this kind was discredited because there was insufficient recognition that pupils need experience and skill in creating drama in order to do it well. Exposition needs to be seen as part of the content and meaning of the work.

In the following example, 14-year-old pupils had been given the task of preparing a small-group drama based on Voznesensky's poem *First Ice*. A full account of the lesson is given in *Starting Drama Teaching*. Interestingly, the group interpreted the poem not as an account of the break-up of a relationship but as an expression of a tension and rift between mother and daughter, with the latter being unable to confide in her mother. A transcript of the opening of the polished improvisation follows:

Enter Julie and Lindsay from left.

JULIE: Mam, mam . . . mam . . . she didn't wait for us again, mam.
MOTHER: Did she not?
JULIE: No.
MOTHER: (*Looking firmly at Lindsay.*) What did she not wait for?

The use of the word 'again' suggests a recent past, and some ongoing problem. The repetition of 'mam' establishes immediately the relationship and the likely respective ages of the daughters.

JULIE: I drew you a picture – that's you, that's your hair, there's the sun and that's our Lindsay.

LINDSAY: Mum, I've got something to tell you.

MOTHER: That's lovely. What did you get for it?

JULIE: A gold star and a tick and a good. And the gold star's gone up on the star chart.

MOTHER: How many have you got now then?

LINDSAY: Mum, are you listening?

JULIE: Four.

MOTHER: Eh, that's good.

LINDSAY: Mum, are you listening?

MOTHER: Mmmm (*looking at the picture*).

LINDSAY: Would you go upstairs for a minute.

JULIE: No.

Mother's reaction and look indicate whose side she is taking.

Lindsay three times says she has something to tell – the repetition indicates that it is likely to be important. She is ignored. The central theme is now coming to the fore.

If there was any doubt about Julie's age, this is now confirmed by the information we get about school.

The specific details about the picture and the rewards are less relevant in themselves but they are part of the exposition because they are providing the focus for the mother to ignore her older daughter.

Lindsay's request for privacy draws even more attention to the fact that she has something to say, but it is part of the restraint of the expository process here that the audience is not told what it is she wants to say.

The opening lines of the drama establish the relationships and the central theme of the play with considerable economy. There is, of course, a danger of creating artificiality by drawing pupils' attention explicitly to techniques of exposition. Dialogue between characters (one of whom needs the same information as the audience), telephone calls, use of minor characters, self-revelatory monologues can all appear self-conscious if employed too deliberately. For that reason, techniques of exposition can be specifically explored and practised in the context of script-writing exercises. In each of the following examples the pupils are simply asked to write the opening scene in a way which would convey the necessary information with some subtlety:

- A gang of four are planning to kidnap the daughter of a rich business man and demand a ransom. Two members of the gang are rivals – each thinking he/she should be in charge. A third member has only recently joined the group and has not yet gained the trust of the others. It will be the task of the fourth member to befriend the young girl and lure her to the house rather than abduct her on the street.

- A family reunion is taking place in a large mansion involving the mother of the family (who owns the house and whose husband died some years previously), one son and his wife, a daughter and her fiancé. The wife and fiancé happened to have had a relationship some years earlier which the other characters do not know about. The two children know that their mother has recently changed her will, but they do not know how.
- A group of three scientists are secretly working on a project which will render human beings invisible. They have had some success with animals but two of them feel it is now time to experiment on humans. Two volunteers arrive in response to a newspaper advertisement which has not specified the nature of the experiment. One of the scientists has some doubts about the ethics of proceeding at this stage.

At a superficial level, exposition is simply a process of deciding how information should be given to the audience. At a deeper level, it involves pupils in exploration and decisions about dramatic structure.

CHAPTER SEVEN

Externalising Inner Conflict

FAUSTUS.	. . . These metaphysics of magicians
	And necromantic books are heavenly;
	Lines, circles, letters, and characters:
	Ay, these are those that Faustus most desires.
	O, what a world of profit and delight,
	Of power, of honour, of omnipotence,
	Is promis'd to the studious artisan!
	All things that move between the quiet poles
	Shall be at my command: emperors and kings
	Are but obey'd in their several provinces,
	Nor can they raise the wind or rend the clouds;
	But his dominion that exceeds in this
	Stretcheth as far as doth the mind of man:
	A sound magician is a demi-god;
	Here tire, my brains, to get a deity!

Enter WAGNER.

	Wagner, commend me to my dearest friends,	
	The German Valdes and Cornelius;	
	Request them earnestly to visit me.	
WAGNER.	I will, sir.	*Exit.*
FAUSTUS.	Their conference will be a greater help to me	
	Than all my labours, plod I ne'er so fast.	

Enter the ANGEL *and* SPIRIT.

GOOD ANGEL.	O Faustus, lay that damned book aside
	And gaze not on it lest it tempt thy soul
	And heap God's heavy wrath upon thy head.
	Read, read the scriptures; that is blasphemy.

BAD ANGEL.   Go, forward, Faustus, in that famous art
                Wherein all nature's treasury is contain'd:
                Be thou on earth as Jove is in the sky,
                Lord and commander of these elements.   *Exeunt* ANGELS.

                *   *   *

Enter the two ANGELS.

BAD ANGEL.   Go forward, Faustus, in that famous art.
GOOD ANGEL. Sweet Faustus, leave that execrable art.
FAUSTUS.   Contrition, prayer, repentance, what of these?
GOOD ANGEL. O, they are means to bring thee unto heaven.
BAD ANGEL.   Rather illusions, fruits of lunacy,
                That make men foolish that do use them most.
GOOD ANGEL. Sweet Faustus, think of heaven and heavenly things.
BAD ANGEL.   No, Faustus, think of honour and of wealth.
                                    Exeunt ANGELS.

                *   *   *

GOOD ANGEL. O Faustus, if thou hadst given ear to me,
                Innumerable joys had follow'd thee;
                But thou didst love the world.
BAD ANGEL.   Gave ear to me,
                And now must taste hell's pains perpetually.
GOOD ANGEL. O, what will all thy riches, pleasures, pomps
                Avail thee now?
BAD ANGEL.   Nothing but vex thee more,
                To want in hell, that had on earth such store.

                           Christopher Marlowe, *Doctor Faustus*

Commentary

The first and third extracts in which the good and bad angels appear are from the beginning and end of the play; the second extract occurs in Scene v when the pact Faustus makes with Lucifer is about to be sealed. The angels first enter during Faustus' opening speech when he expresses his dissatisfaction with the limits of the learning he has so far accomplished and contemplates the delights which await him if he turns to magic. Moments later in the scene when he informs his friends Valdes and Cornelius that he has made up his mind to follow that course of action, he tells them, 'Know

53

that your words have won me *at last*.' (my italics). The use of the phrase *at last* suggests that Faustus has been struggling with his conscience, although this is not a strong feature of his initial speech.

The good and bad angels are the external manifestations of the conflict which we are told Faustus has experienced but which does not feature strongly in the drama until they appear. By using them to give expression to Faustus' inner struggle, the dramatic effect is to allow the long beginning speech to concentrate on the limits of his knowledge and the attractions of what lies ahead. For Faustus himself to dwell on the dangers and evils of what he is contemplating would reduce the ambitious, expansive, soaring opening speech which is an essential part of the ambiguity of the play. The nature of the opening speech contributes to the view that Marlowe at the very least enlists our sympathy for Faustus if not presenting him as hero.

The good and bad angels, however, can be seen not just as manifestations of Faustus' inner struggle but representatives of the real external forces of good and evil, heaven and hell. Thus when they appear at the end of the play they are reminders of the reality which exists outside Faustus. It is the bad angel who presents Faustus with the 'vast perpetual torture-house which is hell'. The emphasis on the external elements allows us to view the play more as an orthodox Christian allegory of the struggle between good and evil.

When the good and bad angels appear in Scene v the sense of genuine internal conflict is more acutely felt. We see Faustus suspended between two courses of action. His echoing the words of the angels reinforces the notion that they are a manifestation of his subjective decision-making. Yet they also represent the external reality of good and evil. The technique used by Marlowe here has its origins in medieval drama but it is employed by him with more subtlety. The angels can be seen to represent both objectivity and subjectivity which is important to the overall meaning of the play. It is necessary to establish the nature of Faustus' inner struggle to give depth to his character, but it is also important to establish the reality of the consequences of his choice in order to emphasise the importance of his decision. 'If we contend that Marlowe felt a profound sympathy for his hero and that he acquiesced in that hero's fall, we are merely arguing that he conceived his play as a genuine tragedy' (Jump, 1962: xlvii).

Of course the manner in which the angels are depicted on stage in production may contribute to the way the audience interprets their function in the play. In a production at the Old Vic in 1961 they appeared high above Faustus as if suspended in the air, stressing their existence as external entities. In Ian McKellan's portrait of Faustus as a 'mental invalid' the two angels were presented as glove puppets on his hand (Bevington and Rasmussen, 1993: 58).

The technique embodies an essential ingredient of dramatic art whereby subjectivity is rendered objective in action. Drama can be described as a concrete and objective art form but the relationship between subjectivity and objectivity works both ways. This is expressed succinctly in the context of a discussion of Hegel's theory of aesthetics, 'The drama is the most dialectical of poetic forms because it exhibits both subjective becoming objective (the character's action constituting the dramatic world) and the objective becoming subjective (the world giving rise to individual expression)' (Cooper 1992: 187).

One of the differences between drama and the novel is the absence in the former of a clear authorial voice or of easy access to characters' inner thoughts. Dramatists seek to overcome this limitation by various devices such as asides, soliloquies, direct address to the audience; but the limitation is also a strength in that the power of drama lies in its concrete objectivity in action. That is why externalising inner conflict is most usefully seen not merely as an expression of inner thoughts.

Examples

This extract can itself be used as an exercise in staging by asking the class to determine how the angels would be represented, how they would be depicted, where they would stand in relation to Faustus. Could the scene be staged in different ways to imply either that the conflict is very much internal to Faustus (a more contemporary interpretation) or that the angels represent the external forces of good and the devil? The technique can be used with just two pupils representing the different points of view or with the class articulating different aspects of the dilemma. The extracts exemplify a technique in drama which is effective because of its very simplicity.

Representing conflict can be a useful concrete way of taking stock of key moments in dramatic texts. At the climax of *The Crucible* in Act Four Proctor is hesitating over whether to sign a confession that he was involved in witchcraft. A summary of the conflicting influences on him illustrates that the dramatic situation is more complex than at first might seem. Factors likely to be weighing on his mind in favour of confessing include the following: he will die if he does not confess, his wife wants him to live, his wife is pregnant, many others in the town have confessed, he does not want to project himself as a saint. Against confessing, relevant factors include: he does not wish to give his captors the satisfaction, he knows it is wrong, he knows his wife would not confess, he knows he will lose his integrity and his good name. Unless we have a grasp of the complexity of the drama at this point, it is hard to understand Proctor's sudden refusal to sign his confession because of what appears to be a technicality. The drama is rendered all the more powerful because Proctor, having signed the confession, snatches it back:

> PARRIS: Proctor, the village must have proof that –
>
> PROCTOR: Damn the village! I confess to God, and God has seen my name on this! It is enough!
>
> DANFORTH: No, sir, it is –
>
> PROCTOR: You came to save my soul, did you not? Here! I have confessed myself; it is enough!
>
> DANFORTH: You have not con–
>
> PROCTOR: I have confessed myself! Is there no good penitence but it be public? God does not need my name nailed upon the church! God sees my name; God knows how black my sins are! It is enough!

The extract indicates that the motivation of Parris and Danforth could also be subjected to analysis in the same way, exploring to what degree they are more concerned with religious or political considerations.

The central dilemma which drives Miller's *All My Sons* took place before the action of the play starts. Joe Keller was responsible with his partner for selling defective aeroplane parts, a crime which resulted in his partner being imprisoned but for which he went free. To view Joe purely as a villain, however, is to miss the point of the play which dramatises the myopic loyalty to his own family which narrowed his sense of moral responsibility. This can best be explored by examining the different pressures which might have weighed on Joe at the time he allowed the engine parts to be sold.

The technique can also be employed to examine a particular speech in a play. Many Shakespearean soliloquies can be presented in the form of dilemmas with conflicting demands and considerations pressing on the protagonist. Hamlet's 'To be or not to be . . .' speech lends itself to expression in the form of a conflict between two courses of action. Macbeth's soliloquy, 'If 'twere done when 'tis done..' in which he expresses his uncertainty about killing the king can be set against the pressures which are pointing him in that direction.

In the Introduction it was suggested that one of the ways drama illuminates human experience is paradoxically by simplifying in order to reveal some of its complexities. In reality, internal conflict is experienced in more complex ways than is implied by the simple technique of giving voice to alternative courses of action or pressures on decision making. In life people who are faced by a difficult decision do not necessarily have a firm grasp of alternative courses of actions and reasons for taking one or the other. The inner conflict experienced in those situations is often *felt* as chaotic uncertainty without a logical analysis of possible choices. The externalising process is not therefore necessarily the same as the technique of thought-tracking whereby the actual thoughts of a character are spoken aloud. The technique can be a means of going beyond the bounds of awareness of the individual character at that point in the play – more akin to an expression of the audience's perception or an articulation of what is felt by the character.

Externalising inner conflict in this way can be used as a starting point for drama, as a means of bringing clarity to an ongoing drama in order to crystallise possible courses of action, or as a way of slowing the action down in order to emphasise and summarise central dilemmas.

Examples illustrating some of the various possibilities

- A teenager is deciding whether to leave home or not and her conflicting thoughts are externalised. Following the example in *Faustus*, these can be spoken by the parents on one side and friends on the other, or can be represented by disembodied voices which represent the externalisation of the individual's conflict of feeling. As a starting point for drama, the process of articulating the thoughts sets the context in a way which seeks to explore complexities rather than presenting a one-sided view. The conflict may derive from feelings of responsibility to a young brother, or from the uncertainties and dangers which lie ahead.
- A managing director is deciding whether to sack an employee who has a dependent family but who has been found stealing. The technique is equivalent here to giving two sides of an argument, but it is given more dramatic impact by representing the dilemma in the form of voices speaking directly to the individual. On the surface, the manager may have to weigh up the humanitarian arguments against the risks of setting a dangerous precedent if he is lenient. At a deeper level there may be other factors at work: he himself was given a second chance in similar circumstances at an early stage in his career, or he knows that he is perceived as a soft touch by some of his colleagues.
- Dwellers who live beside a dormant volcano have to decide whether to leave the village or risk staying. Here the conflict is expressed not as

belonging to one individual alone but as part of the collective dilemma facing the villagers. As a starting point, the technique might elicit tension which can provide the focus for the drama – How reliable is the information that the volcano is in danger of erupting? Does anyone have ulterior motives for providing misleading information?

- In a modern drama based on the Pied Piper, the conflicting influences working on the mayor at the point when he has to decide whether to pay the agreed sum of money are articulated aloud. This exercise might be a useful preliminary to enacting a town council meeting at which the decision will be taken. It can also explore whether the mayor might have had any genuine motives for reneging on his promise.

- A small city's finances will be regenerated by the building of a large leisure centre. One of the senior officials involved in the project discovers that the local water is polluted. He discovers that the pollution is being caused by a factory which his own family owns. The scenario, which is derived from Ibsen's *Enemy of the People,* lends itself to an externalisation of the conflict and dilemma faced by the central character.

Pupils can be taught to incorporate this non-naturalistic technique into their own group plays which very often will include internal conflicts.

CHAPTER EIGHT

False Identity

MR FOWLER *has come into the hotel lounge.*

MRS RAILTON-BELL: Ah, Mr Fowler, good. Would you take a seat, and then we can begin. The two young people are in a hurry. I'm afraid I have very grave news for you all.

CHARLES: The boiler's gone wrong again?

MRS RAILTON-BELL: No. I only wish it were something so trivial.

CHARLES: I don't consider shaving in cold, brown water trivial.

MRS RAILTON-BELL: Please, Mr Stratton.

MR FOWLER: (*Anxiously.*) They're raising the prices again?

MRS RAILTON-BELL: No. My news is graver even than that.

MR FOWLER: I don't know what could be graver than that.

MRS RAILTON-BELL: The news I have to give you, Mr Fowler.

CHARLES: Look, Mrs Railton-Bell, must we play twenty questions? Can't you just tell us what it is?

MRS RAILTON-BELL: (*Angrily.*) My hesitation is only because the matter is so painful and so embarrassing for me that I find it difficult to choose my words. However, if you want it baldly, you shall have it. (*After a dramatic pause.*) Major Pollock – who is not a major at all but a lieutenant promoted from the ranks in the R.A.S.C. –

CHARLES (*Excitedly.*) No. You don't say! I knew it, you know. I always knew Sandhurst and the Black Watch was a phoney. Didn't I say so, Jean?

JEAN: Yes, you did, but I said it first – that night he made the boob about serviettes.

MR. FOWLER: (*Chipping in quickly.*) I must admit I've always slightly suspected the public-school education. I mean only today he made the most shocking mistake in quoting Horace – quite appalling.

MRS RAILTON-BELL (*Raising her voice.*) Please, please, ladies and gentlemen. This is not the point. The dreadful, the really ghastly revelation is still to come.

She gains silence and once again pauses dramatically.

He was found guilty –

LADY MATHESON: Pleaded guilty –

MRS RAILTON-BELL: Please, Gladys. He was found or pleaded guilty – I don't really see that it matters which – to behaving insultingly to no less than six respectable women in a Bournemouth cinema.

There is an aghast silence.

CHARLES (*At length.*) Good God! What a performance.

LADY MATHESON: Really, Maud, I must correct that. I must. We only know one was respectable – the one who complained – and even she seemed a little odd in her behaviour. Why didn't she just say straight out to the Major: 'I do wish you'd stop doing whatever it is that you are doing'? That's what I'd have done. About the other five we don't know anything at all. We don't even know if he nudged them or anything.

Terence Rattigan, *Separate Tables*

*   *   *   *

OTHELLO:	'Tis pitiful: but yet Iago knows
	That she with Cassio hath the act of shame
	A thousand times committed; Cassio confess'd it,
	And she did gratify his amorous works,
	With the recognizance and pledge of love,
	Which I first gave her; I saw it in his hand,
	It was a handkerchief; an antique token
	My father gave my mother.
EMILIA:	O God, O heavenly God!
IAGO:	Zounds, hold your peace!
EMILIA:	'Twill out, it will: I hold my peace sir, no,
	I'll be in speaking liberal as the air,
	Let heaven, and men, and devils, let 'em all,
	All, cry shame against me, yet I'll speak.

William Shakespeare, *Othello*

Commentary

Although at first sight the two extracts seem to have little in common, they both hinge on the revealing of information about a dramatic figure which has, until that point in the play, been concealed.

Rattigan's play centres on the unmasking of Major Pollock and the reactions of the other long-term residents in the hotel in which they are staying. At the start of the extract Mrs Railton-Bell sets out to deliver the truth about him but this only emerges several exchanges later. The delay in delivering the news has some comic import ('They're raising the prices again') but also is a source of tension. The withholding of the information adds to the dramatic effect and focuses the audience on what from now on will be one of the play's central concerns. The audience have already witnessed the uncovering of his real identity and background, revealed through the simple device of a newspaper article which he is at pains to keep from the residents. Now that the other residents also know the truth, the source of the dramatic tension changes. What will be central to the play from this point onwards will be the reactions of the other characters and the moral implications of their judgements.

The Major's attempt to project himself as someone of a higher social status also gives rise to a degree of humour as the residents assume that this is the extent of the revelation. His social *faux pas* cause as much excitement as the darker revelations about his character. Mrs Railton-Bell who is all too eager to spread the gossip is disingenuous in her declaration that this is all too embarrassing to her. One way of interpreting her actions in this extract is to see her as seeking to create another 'false identity' for the Major. She is all too ready to exaggerate his misdemeanour and present it in the worst possible light. The more reasonable Lady Matheson tries to balance her interpretation, drawing attention to the fact that he pleaded guilty and pointing out that some facts of the case are still not known and might reduce the extent of his crime.

The unfolding drama focuses on the reactions of the residents and the second 'trial' of the Major as they decide whether he should be asked to leave the hotel. Another central theme is the relationship between the Major and Mrs Railton-Bell's daughter Sybil who has never married, being dominated and given no space for personal maturity and growth by her mother. Whereas the Major has been creating for himself a false identity, Sybil has been unable to establish for herself an identity independent from her mother. In the final scene the repressed daughter defies her mother by refusing to ignore the Major. He decides to remain in the hotel rather than go somewhere else where he knows he will have to establish another false persona, 'I don't like myself as I am, I suppose, so I've had to invent another person'.

Ironically the hotel is called 'Beauregard', underlining the contrast between illusion and reality which is at the heart of this play. The play

Separate Tables is made up of two one act pieces. Both are set in the same hotel and have characters in common, with the male protagonists taking refuge in false identities in each. In the first play the central male character has adopted a new identity after his promising political career was shattered by his imprisonment for assault.

The extract from Othello is from the final act when Iago's true character is about to be revealed. Although disguise is not used, the notion of false identity and the contrast between appearance and reality is of major importance in the play. Until this point Iago is trusted by Othello, while Cassio and Desdemona are both falsely accused. In Othello's final meeting with Iago not only is he disclaiming his own identity but he is questioning Iago's.

> LODOVICO: Where is this rash and most unfortunate man?
> OTHELLO: That he that was Othello – here I am.
> LODOVICO: Where is that viper? Bring the villain forth.
> OTHELLO: I look down towards his feet – but that's a fable.
> If thou be'st a devil, I cannot kill thee. (*Wounds Iago.*)

The audience have been aware of the deceit from the beginning so the dramatic irony throughout the play is intense.

The notion of 'false identity', then, is being used in this chapter to refer both to the assumption of a different persona through disguise and to the false perception of a character's true moral worth. The adoption of disguise was central to much Elizabethan and Jacobean drama and fulfilled a variety of purposes: it was often a means of resolving plot, it allowed a banished character to return to the action, it was used as a means whereby characters discovered more about themselves (Banks 1991: 150). In *King Lear* Kent is able to return in disguise to serve his master while Edgar finds safety in the role of Poor Tom. The device, however, is not merely functional; the question of identity is central. Lear asks early on 'Who am I?' and receives from Oswald the answer 'My Lady's father'; when he asks 'Who is it that can tell me who I am?' the Fool replies, 'Lear's shadow.' Lear's redemption corresponds with self-knowledge and the recognition of man's essential nature.

Of course all drama is an illusion so that the adoption of a disguise or false identity is to create an illusion within an illusion. When a character adopts a role we are witnessing an actor pretending to be someone else who in turn is pretending to be someone else. The use of disguise or false identity draws attention to an essential element of all drama. This is described very clearly by O'Neill (1995: 83) who suggests that functional roles can acquire complexity by requiring characters to role-play within

their roles, '. . . the single most powerful dramatic constraint in both theatre and process drama is the kind of concealment and disguise offered by
role-playing within the role. It is precisely here that the double nature of
theatre is most clearly at work. Playing a role is the means by which the
very concept of role itself is investigated.'

Examples

From this discussion it can be seen that the use of the notion of 'false
identity' in pupils' own drama can take a number of forms. It may refer to
the unmasking of a person who is guilty of a crime, as in the case of the
'whodunit'. In this case the true identity of the individual in question may
be concealed from both the other figures in the drama and the audience. It
may take the form of disguise of which the audience have knowledge so
that the drama is heavily laden with irony. It may refer to identity rather
than physical disguise so that the centre of interest is on the revelation of
true character.

The structural and thematic focus of the drama may centre on the question of identity from the start. Alternatively the introduction of doubt
about a particular person in a drama is a method some teachers use to
introduce tension:

- In a drama about an escape from prison the question arises, 'How can
  we be sure that someone in our group will not betray us?' This sort of
  intervention was common in 'living through' drama but can equally be
  used in pre-planned work.
- A drama which parallels Miller's *The Crucible* has as its centre uncertainty about whether the teenage girls are in fact guilty of dabbling in
  witchcraft or not. In Bolton's lesson on this theme which is described
  by O'Neill (1995: 35) the pupils are asked to determine their own guilt
  or innocence outside the drama which is only revealed at the end.
- A play about a stranger arriving in a village has as its initial focus
  doubts about the newcomer's real identity. He/she may have a past
  which is associated with the village or there may be designs on some
  wealth or resource.
- With a young class of nine/ten year olds the focus of the drama is
  on determining whether the man who lives in the house outside the
  village (teacher in role) is really a wizard.
- With teacher in role as a tramp who has lost his memory, the challenge
  for the pupils is to establish his identity from the belongings he carries
  in his bag and to help him recall his past.

The following drama took as its starting point a minor character in Roald Dahl's *Danny the Champion of the World*. The class teacher had asked a group of PGCE student teachers who were going to work with the class of ten/eleven year olds to base the drama on Captain Lancaster, using him simply as a starting point. He appears briefly in the novel as a typical Roald Dahl caricature adult – a vicious, strict, unreasonable teacher. The lack of depth in the character as he is depicted in the novel presented a challenge for the creation of the drama, and the solution was to create a more complex persona. The lesson took the following sequence:

1. The pupils watched a tableau created by the teachers of a moment in the novel in which Captain Lancaster appeared. Their task was simply to guess what scene from the novel was being depicted. This activity provided an introduction which engaged their interest, gave them success and provided a focus for some initial discussion of the character. It also provided an example of tableaux which would be helpful when they were asked later to create their own.

2. The pupils in groups were given a series of adjectives on cards and were asked to choose ones which they thought described the Captain accurately as he is depicted in the book. These were placed inside a large outline of a body (representing the Captain) which had been cut out and placed on the wall.

3. Pupils were then asked to watch a very simple piece of mimed drama. One teacher playing the role of Captain Lancaster left school, walked stiffly down the road, went into his house and immediately relaxed the tension in his body. He then proceeded to mime the opening of a cage and the taking out of a pet (a rabbit) which he fondled and then fed. The initial challenge for the pupils was to guess what was going on.

4. The mime sequence raised the question: Is there more to Captain Lancaster than meets the eye? The pupils decided that, among other methods, one way to find out more about him would be to interview characters who knew him from his present and past. Teachers had already been briefed to anticipate this as one of the suggestions and had prepared roles of people who had at some time had an association with him (a former girlfriend, a superior in the army, a neighbour, etc.)

5. Pupils interviewed teachers in role as the friends and acquaintances from Captain Lancaster's past and present life which filled in the background to a much more complex character. It was not a question of providing a romanticised version which depicted him as really a kind and pleasant person: what emerged was a far more complex and ambiguous picture.

6. Pupils now chose more adjectives to place inside the cut-out character and decided whether ones already there should be omitted. They also placed them above or below a dividing line on the template according to whether the words described his private or public face.
7. The next stage was for the pupils to create tableaux and then enact small-group plays which aimed to show another side to Captain Lancaster's character which was certainly not on show in school.

The drama centred on the concept of uncovering the real identity, not in the sense of replacing one simplistic version with another, but of creating more complexity and depth.

CHAPTER NINE

Framing Action

The common room of Proctor's house.

At the right is a door opening on the fields outside. A fireplace is at the left, and behind it a stairway leading upstairs. It is the low, dark, and rather long living-room of the time. As the curtain rises, the room is empty. From above, ELIZABETH *is heard softly singing to the children. Presently the door opens and* JOHN PROCTOR *enters, carrying his gun. He glances about the room as he comes toward the fireplace, then halts for an instant as he hears her singing. He continues on to the fireplace, leans the gun against the wall as he swings a pot out of the fire and smells it. Then he lifts out the ladle and tastes. He is not quite pleased. He reaches to a cupboard, takes a pinch of salt, and drops it into the pot. As he is tasting again, her footsteps are heard on the stair. He swings the pot into the fireplace and goes to a basin and washes his hands and face.* ELIZABETH *enters.*

ELIZABETH: What keeps you so late? It's almost dark.

PROCTOR: I were planting far out to the forest edge.

ELIZABETH: Oh, you're done then.

PROCTOR: Aye, the farm is seeded. The boys asleep?

ELIZABETH: They will be soon. (*And she goes to the fireplace, proceeds to ladle up stew in a dish.*)

PROCTOR: Pray now for a fair summer.

ELIZABETH: Aye.

PROCTOR: Are you well today?

ELIZABETH: I am. (*She brings the plate to the table, and, indicating the food*) It is a rabbit.

PROCTOR (*going to the table*): Oh, is it! In Jonathan's trap?

ELIZABETH: No, she walked into the house this afternoon; I found her sittin' in the corner like she come to visit.

PROCTOR: Oh, that's a good sign walkin' in.

ELIZABETH: Pray God. It hurt my heart to strip her, poor rabbit. (*She sits and watches him taste it.*)

PROCTOR: It's well seasoned.

ELIZABETH (*blushing with pleasure*): I took great care. She's tender?

PROCTOR: Aye. (*He eats. She watches him.*) I think we'll see green fields soon. It's warm as blood beneath the clods.

ELIZABETH: That's well.

(*Proctor eats, then looks up.*)

PROCTOR: If the crop is good I'll buy George Jacob's heifer. How would that please you?

ELIZABETH: Aye, it would.

PROCTOR (*with a grin*): I mean to please you, Elizabeth.

ELIZABETH (*it is hard to say*): I know it, John.

(*He gets up, goes to her, kisses her. She receives it. With a certain disappointment, he returns to the table.*)

PROCTOR (*as gently as he can*): Cider?

ELIZABETH (*with a sense of reprimanding herself for having forgot*): Aye! (*She gets up and goes and pours a glass for him. He now arches his back.*)

PROCTOR: This farm's a continent when you go foot by foot droppin' seeds in it.

ELIZABETH (*coming with the cider*): It must be.

Arthur Miller, *The Crucible*

Commentary

This extract opens the second act of Miller's play. In the first act, amidst the pandemonium and hysteria caused by what is thought to be the outbreak of witchcraft in Salem, we have learned that Proctor previously had an affair with one of the young girls, Abigail, while she was a servant in his household. The quiet, domestic scene which opens Act Two is in great contrast to the hysteria which closed Act One but it carries its own underlying tension. Not only does the audience know what happened before between Proctor and Abigail and that she still has designs on him, but they are also aware that Elizabeth had knowledge of the affair and insisted that Abigail leave the household. We are about to see Proctor and Elizabeth together for the first time in the play.

Before any words are spoken, the simple action on stage serves to introduce or 'frame' the scene. The contrast with the hysteria of the end of the previous act is heightened when we hear Elizabeth gently singing to the children. This also emphasises the family context. The gender roles are clearly defined as they would have been at that time – Proctor enters carrying his gun which he places carefully against the wall before he tastes the stew. His displeasure and his act of seasoning the food carries symbolic force, particularly when it is contrasted with the strained politeness of the exchange of the dialogue: 'It's well seasoned'. The petty dishonesty (her footsteps are heard on the stairs and he swings the pot back into place) exists because of the cloud hanging over them. It is a scene of some subtlety because, rather than being critical of each other or arguing, they are busy working self-consciously at their behaviour and dialogue, trying to be sensitive to the other's feelings. The same effect is achieved by Proctor's very ordinary request for cider which again is a source of some discomfort to both of them. Trivial actions take on a deeper significance in the light of knowledge of the wider context.

As the conversation develops after the extract it is not surprising that the subject which has been in the background straining their conversation comes to the fore,

> ELIZABETH: You were alone with her?
> PROCTOR: (*stubbornly*): For a moment alone, aye.
> ELIZABETH: Why, then, it is not as you told me.
> PROCTOR (*his anger rising*): For a moment, I say. The others come in soon after.
> ELIZABETH (*quietly – she has suddenly lost all faith in him*): Do as you wish, then.

The framing action which precedes the dialogue in this scene serves as a prologue to what follows and the simple act of seasoning the stew become a vehicle for encapsulating the tension between husband and wife, and the striving after normality and happiness. Meaning in drama is communicated through 'multimedial' forms (Pfister, 1988). Here the non-verbal code which introduces the scene contributes to the meaning of the dramatic dialogue which follows.

An audience does not come to a theatre performance 'blind'. There are all sorts of ways in which response to the drama is influenced by what happens before the performance: the title of the play, advance notices, design of the set being just some examples of the preparatory indicators which begin to shape the responses to the drama before it begins (Esslin, 1987). By including 'framing action' as one minor example of those indicators, I wish to distinguish between the sorts of action which the director and actors interpret as appropriate for the scene and those which the playwright has specifically called for in the secondary text (the verbal text segments which are not reproduced on stage in spoken form). It is also helpful to distinguish between the more casual scene-setting action and those actions which contribute more substantially to the meaning of what follows. A dramatic figure may be reading a newspaper at the start of a scene but the action itself may be of limited significance.

At the start of *Educating Rita,* Frank, the university lecturer, is seen desperately searching through the books on the shelves in his office until he finally locates under 'Dickens' a whiskey bottle from which he proceeds to pour himself a drink. His drinking is symptomatic of disillusionment with his personal and professional life and informs the audience's perception of his first meeting with Rita. Later in he play he comments, 'the great thing about the booze is that is makes one believe that under all the talk one is actually saying something'. *Rosencrantz and Guildenstern Are Dead* opens with the two main characters betting on the toss of a coin which turn up heads each time. When the dialogue begins, the run of heads continues and prompts them to speculate on the laws of probability or the likelihood of divine intervention. They try to make sense of what happens here just as they try to make sense of their existence. Because Rosencrantz and Guildenstern are characters from a play they live in a universe which is predetermined so that spinning of the coins has more than casual significance. The opening of *Absurd Person Singular* has one of the main characters, Jane, bustling around the kitchen wiping the floor and surfaces, anything in sight, with a cloth. Her fastidious obsession with cleanliness and tidiness is one of the sources of humour in the play as well as contributing to its darker side; in the second act Jane is so absorbed cleaning the oven she fails to notice the emotional plight and farcical attempts at suicide of one of the other characters.

The concept of 'framing action', although very focused and specific (and for that reason a useful topic for exploration with pupils), can lead to consideration of wider questions in drama. Parallels can be drawn with the convention of dumb shows which appeared in early Elizabethan tragedies (and reappear in some of Shakespeare's plays) in which the main action of the play was first represented in mime. Hamlet is dismissive of 'inexplicable dumb shows' (3, 2) and Ophelia describes their limited purpose, 'Belike this show imports the argument of the play'. Attention to framing action is a useful way of opening up the whole area of the inter-relationship between the sign systems in drama and the changing emphasis on different ones in the history of theatre. The absence of visual aspects of the drama – such as set and lighting – which are taken for granted now required much greater reliance on the language. In classical tragedies the verbal codes dominated, so that much of the action happened off-stage (see Chapter 21: Reported Action). Framing action then can be explored in the context of the wider signing systems in drama.

Examples

The extract from *The Crucible* can be used as the stimulus for work on the text itself.

1. If we take the dialogue without any prior knowledge of what happens earlier in the play, and without the framing action and stage directions, it could easily be read as a simple domestic exchange between a married couple. The way Elizabeth delivers the opening question 'What keeps you so late . . . ?' will depend on the context and can express
   • genuine concern and worry
   • mild curiosity but welcome
   • a strong element of accusation
   • considerable anger.

   Pupils can be asked to attempt to enact those possibilities and consider how the precise tone adopted would determine the way the rest of the scene develops.

2. It is a useful extract for working on subtext. Two actors can take the parts of Proctor and Elizabeth while two others intersperse their thoughts between the lines. This is a useful way of considering the characters in more depth because it will not be immediately apparent what their thoughts might be. With the knowledge of what happens before and after this scene, the words of Proctor and Elizabeth have more import, but it is still open to question how they are really viewing each other.

3. Pupils can be asked to try to think of framing action for this scene which would be more appropriate for preceding the establishment of a totally harmonious relationship. For example, instead of tasting the stew and expressing disapproval, he might stand for a moment to listen to his wife's singing before settling himself at the table.

Just as the perception of an audience can be framed by various factors which precede the opening dialogue, it is helpful for pupils to be provided with a 'way in' to the study of a play. The most obvious approach to *The Crucible* is by opening up the theme of witchcraft and moral panic for the pupils. However, an alternative approach might be to concentrate on the relationship between Elizabeth and Proctor, reading the extracts printed here first and asking the pupils to imagine what might have happened during the last meeting between Abigail and Proctor, before turning to Act One to find out.

The technique of framing action can be introduced to pupils as a convention to consider in their own small-group play making or as a way of giving them a starting point for their work, as in the following examples:

- A teenager is leaving home and the scene will centre on a meeting with her more sympathetic parent before she leaves. Before the parent enters her bedroom the teenager slowly packs her bag, examining various items including photographs as she tries to decide what to take. The actions convey her ambivalence and feelings of some regret. From a pragmatic point of view for the pupils, the action is less demanding than dialogue and may help set the right tone for the scene which follows.

- Two old people are planning a birthday surprise for their grandchild but they have little money. The framing action hints at their need to be frugal which is not specifically acknowledged in their dialogue but is an underlying tension. They might, for example, appear at the start of the scene miming the preparation of a paltry meal: opening a tin carefully, pouring half the contents into a saucepan and so on.

- In a drama based on a modern-day version of the Pied Piper, the townsfolk call on the mayor to complain about their plight and the lack of action the council has taken to alleviate the problem with rats. Before they arrive at his office unannounced, the framing action conveys his affluence: he pours himself a drink, lights a cigar and then proceeds to hide both when he hears their knock at the door.

- A family who are about to meet the parents of their future son/daughter in-law convey their nervousness by straightening the furniture, placing and replacing ornaments unnecessarily and shining various surfaces. Their nervousness is not obvious when the visitors first arrive. An alternative is for one of the pair to be active and the other to be casually indifferent, reading the newspaper.

Sometimes the action can be used simply to convey information which one of the characters totally contradicts when the dialogue begins. The request for a loan to be repaid is turned down by one of the characters who claims to have no money. Moments before he was seen counting a large quantity of notes and placing them in a drawer or safe.

An example of this technique occurred in a drama which took as its starting point Roald Dahl's *Danny the Champion of the World* described in more detail in Chapter 8. The aim was to create a more complex character than the stereotypically evil character portrayed in the novel. The actor playing the part of the teacher whose character was the centre of interest walked home, entered his living room visibly relaxing and proceeded to mime the fondling and feeding of a pet rabbit. This immediately complicated his character. The technique provided a means of engaging interest because the pupils had to guess what was going on.

What these examples have in common is that the initial action casts a new meaning on the scene which follows. The method works obliquely through hints and suggestions, creating the potential for subsequent irony and different levels of meaning and interpretation.

CHAPTER TEN

Incongruity

[The scene is a dinner party at a restaurant.]

They are quite drunk. They get the giggles.

MARLENE *notices* GRISELDA.

MARLENE: Griselda! / There you are. Do you want to eat?

GRISELDA: I'm sorry I'm so late. No, no, don't bother.

MARLENE: Of course it's no bother. / Have you eaten?

GRISELDA: No really, I'm not hungry.

MARLENE: Well have some pudding.

GRISELDA: I never eat pudding.

MARLENE: Griselda, I hope you're not anorexic. We're having pudding, I am, and getting nice and fat.

GRISELDA: Oh if everyone is. I don't mind.

MARLENE: Now who do you know? This is Joan who was Pope in the ninth century, and Isabella Bird, the Victorian traveller, and Lady Nijo from Japan, Emperor's concubine and Buddhist nun, thirteenth century, nearer your own time, and Gret who was painted by Brueghel. Griselda's in Boccaccio and Petrarch and Chaucer because of her extraordinary marriage. I'd like profiteroles because they're disgusting.

JOAN: Zabaglione, please.

ISABELLA: Apple pie / and cream.

NIJO: What's this?

MARLENE: Zabaglione, it's Italian, it's what Joan's having, / it's delicious.

NIJO: A Roman Catholic / dessert? Yes please.

MARLENE: Gret?

GRET: Cake.

GRISELDA: Just cheese and biscuits, thank you.

MARLENE: Yes, Griselda's life is like a fairy-story, except it starts with marrying the prince.

GRISELDA: He's only a marquis, Marlene.

MARLENE: Well everyone for miles around is his liege and he's absolute lord of life and death and you were the poor but beautiful peasant girl and he whisked you off. / Near enough a prince.

NIJO: How old were you?

GRISELDA: Fifteen.

NIJO: I was brought up in court circles and it was still a shock. Had you ever seen him before?

GRISELDA: I'd seen him riding by, we all had. And he'd seen me in the fields with the sheep.*

ISABELLA: I would have been well suited to minding sheep.

NIJO: And Mr Nugent riding by.

ISABELLA: Of course not, Nijo, I mean a healthy life in the open air.

JOAN: *He just rode up while you were minding the sheep and asked you to marry him?

GRISELDA: No, no, it was on the wedding day. I was waiting outside the door to see the procession. Everyone wanted him to get married so there'd be an heir to look after us when he died, / and at last he announced a day for the wedding but

MARLENE: I don't think Walter wanted to get married. It is Walter? Yes.

GRISELDA: nobody knew who the bride was, we thought it must be a foreign princess, we were longing to see her. Then the carriage stopped outside our cottage and we couldn't see the bride anywhere. And he came and spoke to my father.

Caryl Churchill, *Top Girls*

Commentary

Griselda is the last to arrive at the restaurant for the dinner party. By the time she gets there the dinner is nearly over and the guests fairly drunk. They have been exchanging stories about their individual histories – not systematically, but interrupting each other and taking cues from what others contribute. One of the unusual features of the first act of the play from which this section is taken is the strangely incongruous mix of characters who are assembled for the dinner. Marlene introduces them in this extract after the audience has already heard much about their backgrounds.

Joan, disguised as a man, was thought to have been Pope between 854 and 856 CE (AD). The Victorian Isabella Bird was the daughter of a clergyman who found it hard to cope with the 'ordinary drudgery of life' (Act One) and found refuge in her travels. Lady Nijo was born in 1258 CE (AD) and became a Buddhist nun after spending the first part of her life as an emperor's courtesan: 'The first part of my life was all sin and the second all repentance'. Gret was the subject of a Brueghel painting and patient Griselda a character from fiction. The latter appears in Chaucer and Boccaccio as the patient wife who was subjected to various tests by her husband to prove her goodness and patience. Three of the women became famous because they usurped roles normally reserved for men, two of them were subject to cruel abuse by men. The exploitation of women which is a theme examined with considerable subtlety in the rest of the play is symbolised in this first act by the presence of the disparate group of women whom the audience is invited to compare.

These oddly assorted characters (one from fiction, one from a painting and three from different periods of history) are the guests of Marlene who has called the dinner party to celebrate her promotion to director of the employment agency for which she works. The incongruity derives not just from the mix of characters but also from the context. The women are not presented in an expressionist style as ghostly voices from the past but as real flesh and blood characters adopting all the mannerisms and conventions of a group having dinner. The exchanges about dessert in this extract which are so characteristic of a dinner table conversation are typical of those which accompany their chatter.

Churchill uses the device of overlapping dialogue in this act which is explained in the notes which accompany the play. When one character starts speaking before the other has finished the point of interruption is marked /.

> MARLENE: Of course it's no bother. / Have you eaten?
> GRISELDA: No really, I'm not hungry.

Griselda starts speaking here as Marlene says 'Have you eaten?' When a speech follows on from one which started earlier the continuity is marked *. The way the speeches overlap reinforces the fact that although the characters converse, they are more concerned to tell their own stories than really listen to each other.

Another effect of the use of overlapping speech is to make the language more naturalistic than that which is usually found in dramatic dialogue. The language of drama tends not to replicate real life speech. Elam (1980) has identified a number of factors which distinguish dramatic and everyday discourse. The former tends to be more syntactically ordered with few of the false starts and repetitions which characterise ordinary conversation. Also in drama there tends to be less attention to the social functions of language which serves merely to establish relationships. Dramatic dialogue is more economical and tends to be 'purer' in that every exchange counts in some way. It also tends to avoid the overlapping of speech and competition to speak which characterises normal conversation. The great degree of naturalism of the language in this extract (as exemplified by the talk about dessert and the interruptions) intensifies the incongruity even more.

It is not just the mix of characters in Act One which challenges normal expectations derived from traditional dramatic forms. There is also an absence of any sense of an unfolding plot. There are however thematic parallels. Marlene is a woman who has achieved power in a man's world. The guests have either achieved power or have been subject to abuse – Joan, Griselda and Nijo all had babies taken from them. The audience will learn at the end of the play of the estrangement of Marlene from her own daughter. There is no creation of a need to know *what* will happen or *how* something will happen which are the more normal expectations of drama.

The rest of the play challenges other expectations of traditional drama in its use of time (see Chapter 23: Time Shift). The final scene of the play takes place chronologically before the others, some 12 months before Marlene's promotion. It also uses juxtaposition of contrasting scenes which do not at first appear to have any obvious connection (see Chapter 4: Counterpoint). The dislocation of time and juxtaposition of scenes challenges straightforward notions of cause and effect. Thus the play as a whole uses a number of different conventions but in this chapter the particular interest is in the element of incongruity and the way in which this technique can feed into other drama projects.

Examples

Incongruity, then, refers to the bringing together of discordant or disparate elements in drama. It will be noticed in the case of Churchill's play that the meaning and symbolic force of the grouping of the characters derives from the fact that they do have *something* in common. Combining unlikely characters in this way is a possible focus in drama for more experienced and older classes. Once it is accepted that the normal boundaries of historical time in fiction and non-fiction can be transgressed, the imagination can soar towards the surreal. Some commentators have criticised the first act of Churchill's play as lacking any real dramatic impact, and it may seem that similar work with participants in drama might be subject to the same shortcoming. However the lack of an obvious source of conflict or tension normally associated with drama is compensated for by the impact derived from incongruity in the mix of characters. The challenge is in creating and sustaining belief in them. For such a project to have depth it is necessary for the group to have some common factor, e.g. people who have been falsely accused (Timothy Evans who was wrongly executed in the 1950s, Donalbain from *Macbeth,* Farynor the baker thought responsible for the Fire of London), or fathers whose children have caused them upset (King Lear, the father of a modern pop star, the father of the Prodigal Son).

To imitate Churchill's technique in this way is a challenging task. However, there is a more common form of work using a similar principle which might be termed 'documentary drama'. Here a historical or fictional event is examined through the frame of a group of people making a television documentary about it. The incongruity here derives from the mix of time contexts; modern technical resources and conventions are used to investigate events at the time they happened, using a modern perspective. Pupils are familiar enough with media conventions and styles and readily adapt to the demands of this technique. By deliberately exploiting incongruity the drama can be liberated from the type of *faux pas* that one might expect pupils to make in a project of this kind ('they wouldn't have cars in medieval times') without in any way diminishing the potential for learning in the work.

A drama documentary on the Fire of London supposedly made two or three weeks after the event but using modern resources can use the documentary evidence from the time, such as diary accounts, letters, public records, contemporary prints, to create the programme (Milne, 1986). The advantage of the approach is that a mixture of scripted and improvised work can be used, providing various forms of security for different pupils. This type of project can be undertaken as independent small-group work or with different teams of reporters working on different aspects of the project. Either way it might have the following ingredients:

1. An introduction from the television studio setting the scene, describing the devastation and outlining the aims of the programme (e.g. to establish the cause of the fire, to determine whether there was any neglect or to ask whether the authorities acted appropriately). Establishing some purpose is important not just for the historical/educational aims of the project but also to inject an element of tension which will help to provide a plot interest.

It would have grieved the heart of an unconcerned person, to see the sorrowful looks, the pale cheeks, the tears trickling down the eyes . . . to hear the sighs and groans, the doleful and weeping speeches of the different citizens when they were bringing forth their wives (some from their childbed) and their little ones (some from their sickbed) out of their houses and sending them into the country . . . Now the hopes of London are gone . . .

2. Studio interviews with key witnesses such as Farynor, Pepys, Robert Vine, the Mayor. Pupils can be provided with genuine sources to use as a basis for selecting the content and focus.

It was impossible any fire should happen in his house by accident; for he had after twelve of the clock that night gone through every room thereof, and found no fire, but in one chimney . . . which fire he diligently raked up in embers. He affirmed that there was no possibility for any wind [draught] to disturb them; and that it was absolutely set on fire on purpose.

3. Expert opinion on the construction of the houses, the weather conditions, to determine why the fire spread so quickly.

At one of the clock in the morning, there happened to break out a sad deplorable fire in Pudding Lane, near Fish Street hill, which falling out at that hour of the night, and in a quarter of the town so close built with wooden pitched houses, spread itself so far before the day, and with such distraction to the inhabitants and neighbours, that care was not taken for the timely preventing the further diffusion of it, by pulling down houses as ought to have been . . . It fell out most unhappily too, that a violent wind fomented it . . .

4. Outside reports from Pudding Lane where the fire is believed to have started. A dramatic reconstruction of different versions of events of the evening of 1st September, 1666 tries to show what might have happened that night.

Lord's Day. Some of our maids sitting up late last night to get things ready against our feast today, Jane called us up, about three in the morning, to tell us of a great fire they saw in the City. So I rose, and slipped on my nightgown and went to her window and thought it to be on the back side of Mark Lane at the farthest, but being unused to such fires as followed, I thought it far enough off, and so went to bed and to sleep.

5. Interviews with characters

Oh dear Sir . . . it has cost me 20 pounds to remove my goods in porters and carts. If you can send me some money you will highly oblige me, you shall have it again at Michaelmas.

Everybody endeavouring to remove their goods, flinging them into the River or bringing them into lighters [small boats] that lay off. Poor people staying in their houses as long as till the very fire touched them, and then running into boats or clambering from one pair of stair by the waterside to another . . .

Unless the drama project is undertaken with a conscious awareness that a convention is being used, pupils and teacher are likely to be inhibited by the mix of time scales. It is helpful to establish that a modern language idiom is perfectly appropriate (as in the Churchill extract). There is no reason why the incongruity could not be taken further with interviews between a modern fire-fighter and a citizen at the time.

CHAPTER ELEVEN

Irony

Enter MACBETH

LADY MACBETH:	. . . Great Glamis, worthy Cawdor,
	Greater than both by the all-hail hereafter,
	Thy letters have transported me beyond
	This ignorant present, and I feel now
	The future in the instant.
MACBETH:	My dearest love,
	Duncan comes here tonight.
LADY MACBETH:	And when goes hence?
MACBETH:	Tomorrow, as he purposes.
LADY MACBETH:	O never
	Shall sun that morrow see.
	Your face, my thane, is as a book where men
	May read strange matters. To beguile the time,
	Look like the time, bear welcome in your eye,
	Your hand, your tongue; look like th'innocent flower,
	But be the serpent under't. He that's coming
	Must be provided for, and you shall put
	This night's great business into my dispatch,
	Which shall to all our nights and days to come
	Give solely sovereign sway and masterdom.
MACBETH:	We will speak further –
LADY MACBETH:	Only look up clear,
	To alter favour ever is to fear.
	Leave all the rest to me. *Exeunt.*

[*Outside Macbeth's castle*]

DUNCAN:	This castle hath a pleasant seat; the air
	Nimbly and sweetly recommends itself

	Unto our gentle senses.
BANQUO:	This guest of summer,
	The temple-haunting martlet, does approve
	By his loved mansionry that the heaven's breath
	Smells wooingly here. No jutty, frieze,
	Buttress, nor coign of vantage but this bird
	Hath made his pendent bed and procreant cradle;
	Where they most breed and haunt, I have observed
	The air is delicate.

Enter LADY MACBETH

	See, see, our honoured hostess. – The love
DUNCAN:	See, see, our honoured hostess. – The love
	That follows us sometime is our trouble,
	Which still we thank as love. Herein I teach you
	How you shall bid God yield us for your pains,
	And thank us for your trouble.
LADY MACBETH:	All our service
	In every point twice done and then done double,
	Were poor and single business to contend
	Against those honours deep and broad wherewith
	Your majesty loads our house. For those of old,
	And the late dignities heaped up to them,
	We rest your hermits.

William Shakespeare, *Macbeth*

Commentary

This extract from Act 1 Scenes 5 and 6 contains one of the best known examples of irony in drama. Immediately before the entrance of Macbeth the audience witness Lady Macbeth resolve, on receipt of the information that the king has planned to visit them, that King Duncan will not leave the castle alive. Her immediate response to the news that he will enter under her battlements that very night leaves no doubt as to her intentions:

> The raven himself is hoarse,
> That croaks the fatal entrance of Duncan
> Under my battlements . . .

Duncan's words at the start of Scene 6, 'This castle hath a pleasant seat', and Banquo's reference to the 'temple-haunting martlet', which parallels Lady Macbeth's reference to the raven, are highly ironic. Neither Duncan nor Banquo has any idea what the future holds for the king and the words carry more meaning for the audience than for the dramatic figures themselves.

It is helpful to make a distinction between *dramatic irony* and *irony within drama*. The former occurs, as in the example quoted above, when the audience knows more about a situation than the characters on stage. Thus for Duncan to call Lady Macbeth 'our honoured hostess' is in marked contrast to the way the audience views her at this point. The same is true when Banquo declares that 'the air is delicate'. This is ironic in itself but could also be said to contrast with Lady Macbeth's prayer in the previous scene:

> Come, thick night,
> And pall thee in the dunnest smoke of hell . . .

Irony *within* drama occurs when a dramatic figure deliberately makes a statement which carries more than its surface meaning. In this case the dramatic character has ironic intentions. Thus when Lady Macbeth declares that Duncan 'must be provided for' the ambiguity of the phrase and its understated, euphemistic quality renders it a form of irony.

The way Lady Macbeth inveigles her husband to appear as one thing and be another ('look like th'innocent flower, But be the serpent under't') draws attention to the broad irony which is central to the play as a whole. The contrast between appearance and reality, the reversal of what is seen as 'foul' and 'fair', the degree to which the innocent are banished and the guilty trusted and elevated, are all part of the ironic reversal of what is normal or natural which imbues the play as a whole. In the broadest sense of the term, some form of irony is central to all drama in that meaning is invariably at a deeper level than its surface manifestation. Duncan's trust in Macbeth, King Lear's faith in Goneril and Regan, Othello's belief in Iago are all examples of the ironic reversals which are central to the tragedies.

Irony can infuse a whole drama whenever the audience knows the outcome in advance. Tension is created not by wondering what will happen but by seeing how events unfold. Sophocles' *King Oedipus* is a typical example. It is likely that the legends on which much classical drama was based would have been known to the audience. The dialogue in Sophocles' play is heavy with irony because of the audience's knowledge of what has transpired in the past and will happen at the end of the play. Oedipus seeks to learn who caused the previous king's death, unaware that he himself was responsible:

If any of you knows whose hand it was
That killed Laius, the son of Labdacus,
Let him declare it fully, now, to me.
(*He pauses: there is silence*)

The exchange with Tiresias is highly ironic both because it is a blind man (Tiresias) who can see the truth and because later in the play Oedipus will put out his own eyes. States (1994) has claimed that even people who had never heard of the Oedipus legend would know, virtually from the beginning, that Oedipus himself is the killer who is being sought. That knowledge derives from the general expectation the audience brings as audience to the text, alert to the dramatist's potential use of irony, as opposed to any particular knowledge about the content of this play. In other words, if one was observing the scene from the same perspective as the dramatic figures (in much the way one sometimes attempts to solve a murder mystery by seeing things through the eyes of the detective), one would not make the same inference.

Two points are worth making here which are relevant to classroom drama. The first is that it is the spectator's rather than the participant's role which is important in the creation of irony. That does not mean that the drama has literally to have an audience, but the dramatic irony derives from the percipient role (which includes spectator as well as participant). Secondly, irony can derive from the dramatic structure and particularly the use of time shift. If the story of Oedipus were told in a chronological sequence according to the narrative, there would be less potential for irony.

Examples

Clearly the study of irony as it occurs in scripted drama is an important ingredient of drama teaching. I wish to examine some of the ways in which an awareness of the role of irony in drama can also be of value in pupils' own creative work and can inform the teacher's planning and structuring of drama experiences, including choice of approach. In *Starting Drama Teaching* I suggested that in making appropriate choices about the type of work to be undertaken in the drama classroom broad decisions need to be made with respect to orientation (making, performing, responding), organisation (pairs, small group, whole group), mode (script, planned improvisation, unplanned improvisation) and use of conventions. In describing different modes of drama I used the term 'improvisation' as a generic term to include all examples of drama in which pupils work without a script. It is the distinction between planned and unplanned work on which I wish to focus here.

Spontaneous improvisation in which the outcome is not defined in advance has always been highly valued in drama in education because it can provide very rich and emotionally engaging experiences. This way of working is sometimes referred to as dramatic playing, as 'living through' drama or as experiencing the drama in an 'existential' way. The terminology is sometimes confusing but what is central to this method of working is that the outcome is not predetermined. Thus in a drama based on the theme of witchcraft (as an introduction to *The Crucible*) in which a group of villagers turn on one of the members of the community and accuse him of trying to involve the children in sexual practices, the development of events is negotiated as it happens in the drama. I use that example as one which occurred many years ago in a drama with a group of adults for which I was responsible. It left me distinctly uncomfortable and alerted me to the risks involved in this way of working because there is a danger of blurring the distinction between the reality and the fiction (Fleming, 1994: 85).

Irony is less likely to be an ingredient in spontaneous work in drama because the different levels of meaning which it requires more often than not have to be consciously built in. Drama which is carefully crafted and constructed is more likely to have the potential for irony. In the example quoted above in which the villagers make their accusation, a pre-planned scenario might have determined that the person accused was in fact innocent but had been a victim of abuse when he was young. Alternatively, the person leading the accusation might have been the guilty party, or it could have been decided that the rumour had been spread by the children themselves as a cover for their own exploits. What might be lost in the excitement of spontaneous engagement in drama is gained by the potential for creating extra levels of meaning by the injection of ironic undertones.

Irony is more usefully described not so much as a teaching technique or convention but as a way of thinking about the way drama operates at multi levels. More specific, focused examples of dramatic irony sometimes occur in drama which is created by pupils themselves; when they do occur (and they may not necessarily be perceived as ironic by the pupils) it is appropriate for the teacher in discussion to draw attention to them. For example, in the Pied Piper drama, the mayor who has been adamant that the council cannot afford to pay its bill receives a telephone call about an expensive extension to his offices. Later when the townsfolk come to decide whether to pay the Pied Piper the amount promised, they decide that he would be just as happy with thank you letters from the children. This is heavily ironic in the light of what subsequently happens in the tale. In a play about the Fire of London, on the very day the fire started in 1666, the baker Thomas Farynor tells his children about a large fire in London in 1632 (34 years earlier) before putting them to bed.

The concept of dramatic irony can be explored more significantly in exercises specifically designed for the purpose, as in the following examples:

- A teacher is about to admonish a pupil for telling lies. (The pupils might choose to show an additional scene in which the teacher is guilty of the same transgression.)
- A supermarket manager refuses to allow a charity collection outside the store. (The audience learn that a close family relative is deriving benefit from the same charity but the manager does not make the connection.)
- Two teenagers vandalise a public telephone. (They learn later that the broken telephone prevented a friend from receiving medical help.)

Work on scripted extracts in pairs may also be a way of exploring irony in a very simple way using an exercise mode. In each of the following exchanges, pupils can be asked to invent two contexts, one of which is straightforward, the other containing some element of irony (the creation of the context should include who the speakers are, where the exchange takes place and what is happening). The irony can refer simply to one of the lines or to the situation as a whole; it may be a form of dramatic irony or irony within the drama.

A. What time do you call this?
B. I'm sorry I got held up.
A. It's up to you to make sure you get here in time.
B. I'll try not to let it happen again.

The context might be a factory. A worker has arrived late and the boss is telling him/her off. An element of simple irony can be introduced if the boss was also late and only arrived moments before. Alternatively, the context may be school and A is the pupil speaking to the teacher in a humorously ironic manner.

A. Would you like some wine with your dinner, sir?
B. Yes, that would be nice.
A. A dry white would go well.
B. I'd prefer red actually.

The obvious situation is that a waiter is serving at table in a restaurant. The dialogue becomes ironic if the context is changed and they are now two homeless people on the streets sharing half a sandwich and a bottle of milk they have stolen. Alternatively, A might be a wife who has just had a row with B, her husband, because he expects her to wait on him too much.

A. Your mother rang while you were out.
B. What does she want now?
A. She wanted to make sure you were OK.
B. I'll ring her back and tell her I'm fine.

The straightforward context might simply be that A is married to B whose mother fusses about B's health. The exchange becomes rather more sinister if B has earlier been poisoned by his mother. Alternatively, A is actually B's mother and neither of them know this.

A. When will he get in?
B. It shouldn't be long now.
A. I can't wait to surprise him.
B. He'll be delighted.

In the first version A and B have planned a birthday surprise for someone. In the second version A has arrived unexpectedly to visit a family as a surprise, without being aware that none of the family can stand him/her.

The value of introducing irony into pupils' small-group play work can be illustrated by the following example. In a drama about a chemical leak into the water system of a town which will centre on a public enquiry about the incident, the pupils are asked to improvise in small groups scenes which took place before the inhabitants became aware of what has happened. They are given suggestions about possible places the scenes might take place, e.g. outside the supermarket, in the church, in the factory which caused the leak, in the school playground. What the pupils are in effect being asked to do is to prepare an improvisation which has little substance or dramatic tension, there is no real 'peg' on which to hang their work. If the task is set so that now the pupils are required to introduce an element of irony into those scenes, the work will have more depth and be more challenging, e.g. the workers may be expressing fears about or confidence in the safety of the factory; the children may be discussing a homework topic on ecology, the sermon in the church may have ironic resonance.

CHAPTER TWELVE

Mime

As OLD MARTIN *describes their ordeal, the men climb the Andes. It is a terrible progress; a stumbling, tortuous climb into the clouds, over ledges and giant chasms, performed to an eerie, cold music made from the thin whine of huge saws.*

OLD MARTIN: Have you ever climbed a mountain in full armour? That's what we did, him going first the whole way up a tiny path into the clouds, with drops sheer on both sides into nothing. For hours we crept forward like blind men, the sweat freezing on our faces, lugging skittery leaking horses, and pricked all the time for the ambush that would tip us into death. Each turn of the path it grew colder. The friendly trees of the forest dropped away, and there were only pines. Then they went too, and there just scrubby little bushes standing up in ice. All round us the rocks began to whine with cold. And always above us, or below us, those filthy condor birds, hanging on the air with great tasselled wings.

It grows darker. The music grows colder yet. The men freeze and hang their heads for a long moment, before resuming their desperate climb.

Then night. We lay down twos and threes together on the path, and hugged like lovers for warmth in that burning cold. And most cried. We got up with cold iron for bones and went on. Four days like that; groaning, not speaking; the breath a blade in our lungs. Four days, slowly, like flies on a wall; limping flies, dying flies, up an endless wall of rock. A tiny army lost in the creases of the moon.

INDIANS: (*Off: in echo.*) Stand!

The Spaniards whirl round. VILLAC UMU *and his attendants appear, clothed entirely in white fur. The High Priest wears a snow-white llama head on top of his own.*

VILLAC UMU: You see Villac Umu. Chief Priest of the Sun. Why do you come?

PIZARRO: To see the Great Inca.

VILLAC UMU: Why will you see him?

PIZARRO: To give him blessing.

VILLAC UMU: Why will you bless him?

PIZARRO: He is a God. I am a God.

VALVERDE. (*Sotto Voce.*) General!

PIZARRO: Be still.

VILLAC UMU. Below you is the town of Cajamarca. The great Inca orders: rest there. Tomorrow early he will come to you. Do not move from the town. Outside it is his anger.

He goes off with his attendants.

VALVERDE: What have you done, sir?

PIZARRO: Sent him news to amaze him.

VALVERDE: I cannot approve blasphemy.

PIZARRO: To conquer for Christ, one can surely usurp his name for a night, Father. Set on.

Peter Shaffer, The Royal Hunt of the Sun

Commentary

In the text of the play (Act 1 Scene 8) this scene is introduced with the words, 'In the cold night there now ensues: THE MIME OF THE GREAT ASCENT'. This is one of several mimes which, along with the use of ritual, masks and music, was part of Shaffer's aim to create 'a kind of total theatre', as described in the author's notes to the play.

Other epic techniques are also employed. The action is framed throughout by the narration of Old Martin looking back on his participation in the expedition to conquer Peru. In the early part of the play the civilisations of Spain and Peru are deliberately contrasted as the aggressive invaders shatter the tranquillity of the indigenous people and attempt to subjugate them. 'This story is about ruin. Ruin and gold,' announces Martin in his opening speech.

The contrasts in the play are presented not just through the dialogue but through the staging. The frenzied action and marching of the Spaniards is contrasted with the stillness and magnificence of Atahullpa, the sovereign Inca of Peru who appears at the start of Scene Three in the centre of a huge golden sun with twelve great rays, masked, crowned and dressed in gold.

He is contrasted visually with the Conquistador General of the Spaniards. As the play progresses and reaches its climax their similarities are also highlighted.

The scene of the mime of the climbing of the Andes is not simply a way of advancing the plot or of creating a spectacle for its own sake. It relates to the overall meaning of the play and has symbolic import. The climbing of the mountain is an expression of pride, 'There isn't a hill in your whole country a Spaniard couldn't climb'; it represents the physical hardship the men endure in their quest; it also symbolises their aspirations. Pizarro presents himself as a God and it is important that they achieve the climb successfully if that claim is to have any credence. Symbolically the Spaniards have to elevate themselves to reach the sovereign Inca, to reach his level.

The term 'mime' is sometimes used to refer to a deliberate sequence of actions which are intended to convey meaning without language. Alternatively the term can be used simply to refer to one of the sign systems of drama, the gestures which may or may not accompany speech. As Esslin has pointed out, one of the basic differences between a literary and dramatic text is that the latter is always incomplete. Quoting Ingarden, he states that drama represents its world by '(1) events that are wholly indicated by visual and other means, (2) by elements which are indicated both verbally and visually and (3) by events that are indicated only in words, as, for example, narrations of events that have happened outside the spatial or temporal ambit of the action' (Esslin, 1987: 83). He goes on to suggest that the non-verbal categories have primacy over the text: an assassin may speak loving words as he kills his victim.

The distinctions made by Esslin will be useful when considering mime in the context of drama teaching. This ingredient has had a very varied history, occasionally abused, sometimes completely ignored. A lesson can be learned from the use of mime in Shaffer's play because here it is part of the overall aesthetic effect of the work and derives its meaning from the total context. This emphasis on meaning was frequently missing in many early uses of mime in the classroom.

Examples

The term 'mime' tends to refer variously to the separate art form which is 'mime' *per se* (mime artist); to a sequence of actions without speech which is integrated into the drama ('I want you to do this as a mime'); to actions which accompany speech within the drama ('I would like you to mime the appropriate actions as you say the words'); or to separate non-verbal exercises ('Practise throwing a football'). Tableau, which could be described as a form of mime, has for some time been extremely popular in schools but, judging by the literature on the subject, the spoken word has often dominated in the drama classroom to the exclusion of very much specific emphasis on mime or gesture, other than in preliminary warm-up exercises.

Drama in education practice which emerged in the 1970s reacted against what were seen as misguided teaching approaches of the past which concentrated on action to the exclusion of any concern with meaning or attention to content. Frequently children were asked simply to mime actions to accompany the narrative of the teacher as in the following example of a lesson with ten/eleven year olds:

> 'It is early on a summer's morning. Outside the sun is shining. We are asleep in bed; very soon the alarm clock will sound . . .' The children seem asleep – some restlessly, some deeply. The teacher meanwhile has moved imperceptibly over to the stage, and suddenly he rattles a side-drum, and the class reacts – some quite violently. They seem absorbed in the real process of getting out of bed . . . 'Go into the bathroom and have a good wash. Don't forget behind your ears. Clean your teeth and get dressed.'
>
> (Pemberton-Billing and Clegg, 1965: 13)

The lesson continues in that vein with the children contributing little except to translate the narrative into actions. Writing in 1984, I suggested that a key to using mime and focusing on gesture in drama was the context (and overall sense of context of the participants) in which the activities take place. A lesson dealing with 'kings' should involve more than simply asking the class to learn to walk, talk and bow like a king, but might explore questions like, 'How does a king know whom he can trust?', 'What happens to a king who doesn't listen to advice?', 'Does a king have real friends?', 'How do we justify having a king?' Practising the external actions of 'kingship', however, might be a very useful *part* of the lesson, particularly if the way the king walks is related to his power and authority. It is for this reason that decisions about how and when to concentrate on actions can be difficult.

As Bolton has said, 'There are times when even the most careful miming is not enough; at others precision of actions does not matter.' The following uses of mime from his own work provide a helpful insight into when the use of non-verbal actions might be appropriate as a way of starting the drama (Bolton, 1984: 159):

90

Content of drama	Mime
Women waiting for the return of a boat in a drama about a shipwreck.	Sewing a patch on a pair of trousers.
Fourteen-year-old girls who wanted in their drama to be in a 'mad-house'.	The problem of tying shoe laces when concentration is not high.
Ten year olds who wanted to be detectives.	Practising reading a newspaper while watching someone.
Nine year olds taking the part of guards.	Practising marching properly.
Sixteen year olds being old people.	Discovering whether age has affected their handwriting.

These activities all provided a safe way into the topic in question in which the degree of protection was high. Bolton points out that the initial choice of an action like 'sewing a patch on trousers' is not an arbitrary one. "For the teacher this has symbolic overtones to do with the themes of 'waiting', of 'the irony of continuing to patch the clothing of the man who will not return' of the 'intimacy of a husband and wife relationship' of 'the place and duty of a nineteenth-century wife'. . ." (ibid.: 160). Even the example of ten years olds being required to practise marching properly which seems the least dense as an activity could well symbolise the fact that guards have to pay meticulous attention to detail in everything they do. As with the example from Shaffer's play, the key to the use of mime is the context in which it takes place.

Another example, again from Bolton (1992: 70), used mime in a drama sequence based on 'Robin Hood'. After engaging in pairs activity in which a father teaches his son how to make arrows, groups of five or six set up different crafts as a way of building a medieval village. Thus if a family chooses weaving one should tease out the wool, another washes it, another takes the dry wool for spinning and so on. By setting the task in this way the participants were being offered a considerable degree of protection because they were not being asked to 'act' the parts of villagers but to demonstrate physical activities.

Sometimes the action which precedes the dialogue helps to create tension and mood. This was true of many of the examples given in Chapter 9 in the discussion of the use of framing action. A pairs exercise involving a parent and teenager who has promised to be home at a certain time but arrives late is more likely to be successful if the task is set with certain constraints: when the teenager returns the conversation takes place in hushed tones so that the household will not be woken up. It also helps if the teenager actually mimes the deliberate opening of the front door, placing the key carefully in the lock, turning it slowly, relieved to think (mistakenly) that everyone has gone to bed. The drama is not helped if similar attention to detail is given to subsequent actions. If the teenager tries to divert the attention of the parent by making a cup of tea, then this activity is likely to need no more than an indicative gesture.

Mime can be used to build belief and focus concentration. A drama project with seven-year-old children on the theme of pirates used occupational mime as an activity at the start of the lesson, when the children who had been selected as members of the crew demonstrated the skills which they had claimed to have in order to justify being chosen. (Kitson and Spiby, 1995: 43). Here the choice of mime is not arbitrary but is determined by their own earlier decisions. Another drama, again with young children, on the theme of evacuees during the war required the pupils to mime the packing of suitcases just before being evacuated (ibid.: 17). As the pupils perform the mime, their teacher narrates:

> The children took the suitcase down from the wardrobe and opened it. They took the first piece of clothing from the bed and folded it carefully, then put it in the case. Then, just as carefully, they put the rest of the clothes in. As they did so, they wondered what it was going to be like in the new place. Who would they stay with? What sort of house would it be? Would the people like them? . . . Finally they took up one small thing they'd been allowed to take that would remind them of home. They held it in their hands, looking at it, remembering when it was given to them.

At first sight the activity seems similar to the 'summer's morning' example described above in which children mime actions to teacher narration. However there are crucial differences. In this example the mime occurs in a broad, meaningful context which examines the theme of evacuees in some depth. Secondly, there is a strong symbolic dimension in what the children have been required to do – the action of packing the case represents a turning point as they look to the future and the past (see Chapter 3 and the extract from Chekhov). Thirdly, the pace which is set by the narrative slows the action down and creates an appropriate mood.

Mime can also be used in drama when the reason for using nonverbal communication is built into the work. These situations basically are drawing on the familiar game of charades. The intellectual challenge and the 'game' of trying to discover what is being communicated is likely to increase commitment to the work:

- 'A group of children in role as visitors to another planet must show the uncomprehending inhabitants three things about their life on Earth, or demonstrate that they come in peace.' (Kempe, 1996: 41)
- A stranger who has arrived in the village does not speak the same language and his warning about the dangers they face has to be communicated in mime.
- The investigator who returns from the lighthouse has been so shocked by what he has seen that he has been struck dumb and is only able to inform his colleagues on the mainland what he has seen through signs.
- The prisoners in opposite cells are not able to speak to each other but have to find other ways of making their plans.

The examples of the use of mime from contemporary drama lessons illustrate how the technique can be used in order to deepen and advance the drama. At the same time pupils are being given practice in the use of a specific skill, appropriately contextualised.

CHAPTER THIRTEEN

Minimal Context

A country road. A tree. Evening.

Estragon, sitting on a low mound, is trying to take off his boot. He pulls at it with both hands, panting. He gives up, exhausted, rests, tries again. As before.

Enter Vladimir.

ESTRAGON: (*giving up again*). Nothing to be done.

VLADIMIR: (*advancing with short, stiff strides, legs wide apart*). I'm beginning to come round to that opinion. All my life I've tried to put it from me, saying, Vladimir, be reasonable, you haven't yet tried everything. And I resumed the struggle. (*He broods, musing on the struggle. Turning to Estragon.*) So there you are again.

ESTRAGON: Am I?

VLADIMIR: I'm glad to see you back. I thought you were gone for ever.

ESTRAGON: Me too.

VLADIMIR: Together again at last! We'll have to celebrate this. But how? (*He reflects.*) Get up till I embrace you.

ESTRAGON: (*irritably*). Not now, not now.

VLADIMIR: (*hurt, coldly*). May one enquire where His Highness spent the night?

ESTRAGON: In a ditch.

VLADIMIR: (*admiringly*). A ditch! Where?

ESTRAGON: (*without gesture*). Over there.

VLADIMIR: And they didn't beat you?

ESTRAGON: Beat me? Certainly they beat me.

VLADIMIR: The same lot as usual?

ESTRAGON: The same? I don't know.

VLADIMIR: When I think of it . . . all these years . . . but for me . . . where would you be . . . ? (*Decisively.*) You'd be nothing more than a little heap of bones at the present minute, no doubt about it.

ESTRAGON: And what of it?

VLADIMIR: (*gloomily*). It's too much for one man. (*Pause. Cheerfully.*) On the other hand what's the good of losing heart now, that's what I say. We should have thought of it a million years ago, in the nineties.

ESTRAGON: Ah stop blathering and help me off with this bloody thing.

VLADIMIR: Hand in hand from the top of the Eiffel Tower, among the first. We were presentable in those days. Now it's too late. They wouldn't even let us up. (*Estragon tears at his boot.*) What are you doing?

ESTRAGON: Taking off my boot. Did that never happen to you?

VLADIMIR: Boots must be taken off every day, I'm tired telling you that. Why don't you listen to me?

ESTRAGON: (*feebly*). Help me!

VLADIMIR: It hurts?

ESTRAGON: Hurts! He wants to know if it hurts!

VLADIMIR: (*angrily*). No one ever suffers but you. I don't count. I'd like to hear what you'd say if you had what I have.

ESTRAGON: It hurts?

VLADIMIR: Hurts! He wants to know if it hurts!

ESTRAGON: (*pointing*). You might button it all the same.

VLADIMIR: (*stooping*). True. (*He buttons his fly.*) Never neglect the little things of life.

Samuel Beckett, Waiting for Godot

Commentary

This extract which is the opening of Beckett's play provides a minimum amount of contextual information. The setting could not be simpler. The country road suggests the possibility of travel but we never learn where it leads or where the characters have come from. The tree suggests that this is a definite place but the location is never made any more specific. It is not the complete absence of contextual detail (we are given *some* information) but the way it is kept to a minimum which is so intriguing. Much of the extract reads like the beginning of a conventional play with the implication that all will be revealed as the drama unfolds. The fact that a mysterious 'they' who are 'the same lot as usual' beat Estragon suggests some continuity and predictability. In a more conventional play the drama might well centre on the revelation of who 'they' are. However in Beckett's play we never find out. We are given a hint that the characters have a past and an established relationship ('We were presentable in those days'), but we learn very little more about that past.

Vladimir and Estragon are obsessed throughout the play with basic human functions and trivial actions (putting on boots, exchanging hats, etc.). In the context of the wider meaning of the play the utterances in this extract have an ironic meaning; they refer to the trivial happenings but also have a broader significance. 'Nothing to be done' can be judged to refer to the difficulties of putting on the boot as well as to the 'struggle' which is living. 'Hurts!' again refers to the boot and to the pain of existence.

The absence of contextual detail in the play as a whole is central to its meaning. They are waiting for Godot, but we never know who he is, nor is his relationship to the tramps clearly defined. The only other characters who appear, a master and slave and two messengers, are not clearly delineated. The normal expectations of the creation of 'character' in a play do not apply, yet the figures who appear are not presented as mere abstractions – as with Vladimir and Estragon, the audience are given details which individualise the characters but never fully locate or explain them: the boy in Act One is sent from Godot and we learn that he minds the goats and has a brother.

The lack of context in *Waiting for Godot* is central because it isolates the characters in a 'kind of limbo' (Lyons, 1983: 15). The incomprehensibility of the action is precisely because their existence is incomprehensible. The lack of action is paradoxically the central source of the drama which can be seen as essentially a play about the nature of existence. The key here is not the *total* absence of context which would render the dramatic figures mere voices, and an expression of particular ideas. The detail which is provided identifies them as individuals to a degree, makes their humanity palpable and adds to both the tragic and comic impact of the play. For the drama teacher engaged in devising drama with classes, the key questions are how much and what kind of contextual detail is necessary in the construction of drama. Notice these are not questions about exposition (although this is a related issue) but have more to do with the very act of creating the drama.

Examples

In *Starting Drama Teaching* I identified common misconceptions about structuring drama work which derive from two different sources. Knowledge of the capacity pupils have for dramatic play, combined with recognition that pupils adapt to drama very naturally, can lead to an underestimation of the degree of structure pupils need in their work and of the extent to which their skills need to be developed. On the other hand, experience of scripted plays and traditional notions of theatre practice can lead to the assumption that the way to set up drama with pupils (and, equally importantly, the way pupils themselves should initiate drama) is always to cast and create characters and plan a detailed narrative. In fact the degree of contextual detail needed in planning drama activities is often less than is assumed.

Elam (1980: 131) has contrasted the post-Romantic 'psychologistic' view of character with one which sees character as being more a function of dramatic structure and action. The first approach sees "'*dramatis persona*' as a more or less complex network of psychological and social traits; that is as a distinct 'personality'". Some writers prefer the term 'dramatic figure' rather than 'character' because the latter term suggests a level of individuality more akin to the realist novel. 'Figure' on the other hand 'hints at something deliberately artificial, produced or constructed for a particular purpose, and evokes the impression of functionality rather than individual autonomy' (Pfister, 1988: 161). This view of dramatic subjects is not new but has its origins in Aristotle's *Poetics* which asserted the primacy of plot over character.

It is important not to be too dogmatic here. As Aston and Savona have pointed out, clearly some drama texts do have more interest in character *per se* and it is not necessary to choose between a psychological and more functional approach to character. They are not necessarily alternatives: 'The grounding of characterisation in psychological detail need not detract from the structural and ideological functions of character.' (Aston and Savona, 1991: 35). The important practical point is that when setting up drama it is usually not necessary to individualise characters to any great degree; 'character', in as much as it is important, will emerge from the action.

When setting up a drama about the Fire of London a teacher's and pupils' instincts might be to cast individuals in role as the King, Pepys, Lady Hobart, Farynor the baker and so on. Furthermore it might be thought that in order to adopt the part, pupils need to create a character with some depth, e.g. What sort of person is the baker? What relationship does he have with his family, with his customers? How does he treat his employees? etc. However a scene in which, in order to establish his guilt or innocence, the baker is interviewed about the steps and precautions he took on the night of the fire, will neither need elaborate casting or deep characterisation. What is needed for the drama is the adoption of an attitude and the creation of a structure: A is trying to get information from B. The dramatic figure of the baker is a function of the purpose of the drama.

I think this approach to structuring drama can usefully be viewed in terms of the degree of context which needs to be established and is vividly illustrated by examples of setting simple pairs exercise work in drama. Here the creation of tension and supplying motivation is more important than giving details of context. In this case the teacher supplies the outline structure. It is open for the participants to add the minimum necessary details on which to hang the drama (e.g. what the item is in the first example) but the exercises can be attempted without such details being included.

- Someone is returning a faulty item to a shop without a receipt. The shopkeeper thinks it was in perfect condition when it left the shop.
- One friend is trying to inform the other that he/she will not now be able to go on holiday but is finding it hard to get a word in because the other is keen to go over the plans for the holiday.
- A student turns up for the start of a course but finds his/her name not on the list. The course leader has no recollection of interviewing the student.
- A customer is seeking to extend his/her overdraft at the bank. Both manager and customer know each other from their school days but both are at first embarrassed to admit this.
- A shop assistant is being admonished by the boss for being rude to a customer.

As an exercise in drama (I would describe the task as no more than an exercise) it can be fruitful to ask older pupils to attempt to improvise situations in which the absolute minimum of context is defined. At first they find this very challenging and in response to the instruction to improvise 'waiting', the initial instinct is to visualise the scene in a doctor's waiting room or some other concrete situation. However, once the idea is grasped, the exercise, as well as being an interesting 'way into' Beckett's play, also highlights the degree to which context can be minimised and structures highlighted. The same can be attempted with 'persuasion', 'curiosity', 'interference' and so on. The following type of dialogue emerges when 'waiting' improvisations are attempted. The parallel with *Waiting for Godot* is clear.

A. What time is it now?
B. Ten past three.
A. God, isn't it going slowly.
B. We've been here ages.
A. Do you think I should call again?

B. Nobody took any notice the last time.

A. It's so boring all this hanging around.

B. It will be worth it though.

A. You hope.

As has been recognised by a number of writers on drama, the distinction between narrative (the outline of the story) and plot (the structuring of the narrative) is important in creating drama. Partly because their experience of drama often derives from film and television, pupils, left to their own devices, tend to think in terms of complex narrative which they find difficult to translate into dramatic plot. This too can be seen as a matter of deciding on the appropriate degree of context which is required. If we take the final example of one of the simple pairs exercises above, we can see how extra details of context supplied by the teacher need to be related to the development of a dramatic plot rather than simply providing background information. Participants given the simple version of the task to perform may supply such details as what the assistant actually said to cause offence, in which department she was working, and so forth, but the setting of a more complex situation will require different kinds of details.

In the example of a shop assistant who is admonished by the boss for being rude to a customer, the simplest form of structure is that of A accusing B. By adding an extra detail, e.g. a shop assistant *who has only worked in the shop for two weeks* is admonished by the boss for being rude to a customer, the extra information may suggest ignorance (she may not know the procedures or have been trained appropriately) or may imply vulnerability (she could more easily be dismissed).

In another example, a shop assistant who has only worked in the shop for two weeks is admonished by the boss for being rude to a customer *who is known to spend a great deal of money in the shop.* The extra detail here may suggest that her behaviour was justified, that the customer had unreasonable expectations.

Context, then, can be minimised to an extreme degree, as in the case of the exercises which sought to represent 'waiting' and which could, if developed, lead to absurd drama. More often, however, the decision for teachers and pupils is how much and what kind of context is necessary for the creation of the drama. This is less to do with detailed character and background and more to do with carefully selected information which contributes to the dramatic tension.

CHAPTER FOURTEEN

Minor Characters

GERTRUDE: Good (*fractional suspense*) gentlemen . . . .

(*They both bow.*)

He hath much talked of you,
And sure I am, two men there is not living
To whom he more adheres. If it will please you
To show us so much gentry and goodwill
As to expand your time with us awhile
For the supply and profit of our hope,
Your visitation shall receive such thanks
As fits a king's remembrance.

ROS: Both your majesties
Might, by the sovereign power you have of us,
Put your dread pleasures more into command
Than to entreaty.

GUIL: We both obey,
And here give up ourselves in the full bent
To lay our service freely at your feet,
To be commanded.

CLAUDIUS: Thanks, Rosencrantz (*turning to* ROS *who is caught unprepared, while* GUIL *bows*) and gentle Guildenstern (*turning to* GUIL *who is bent double*).

GERTRUDE (*correcting*): Thanks, Guildenstern (*turning to* ROS, *who bows as* GUIL *checks upward movement to bow too – both bent double, squinting at each other*) . . . and gentle Rosencrantz. (*Turning to* GUIL, *both straightening up –* GUIL *checks again and bows again.*)
And I beseech you instantly to visit
My too much changed son. Go, some of you,
And bring these gentlemen where Hamlet is.

(*Two* ATTENDANTS *exit backwards, indicating that* ROS *and* GUIL *should follow.*)

GUIL: Heaven make our presence and our practices
Pleasant and helpful to him.
GERTRUDE: Ay, amen!

(ROS *and* GUIL *move towards a downstage wing. Before they get there,* POLONIUS *enters. They stop and bow to him. He nods and hurries upstage to* CLAUDIUS. *They turn to look at him.*)

POLONIUS: The ambassadors from Norway, my good lord, are joyfully returned.
CLAUDIUS: Thou still hast been the father of good news.
POLONIUS: Have I, my lord? Assure you, my good liege,
I hold my duty as I hold my soul,
Both to my God and to my gracious King;
And I do think, or else this brain of mine
Hunts not the trail of policy so sure
As it hath used to do, that I have found
The very cause of Hamlet's lunacy . . . (*Exeunt – leaving* ROS *and* GUIL.)
ROS: I want to go home.

Tom Stoppard, Rosencrantz and Guildenstern are Dead

Commentary

Stoppard's ingenious work takes two minor characters from *Hamlet* and gives them a life outside the scenes in Shakespeare's play: they talk, toss coins, bicker, play games. *Rosencrantz and Guildenstern are Dead* is built around the action of *Hamlet*. The scenes from Shakespeare's play in which the two characters appear form the backcloth to Stoppard's play in which they try to make sense of what is happening to them. Significant moments from *Hamlet* simply happen in the background and are viewed from the perspective of the minor characters. For example, in Stoppard's play Rosencrantz and Guildenstern are humorously trying to work out how they might make their approach to Hamlet to find out what is wrong with him: 'I can't for the life of me see how we're going to get into conversation.' This is the very point in Shakespeare's play when he is about to deliver the famous soliloquy 'To be or not to be . . .'

Apart from the last line of dialogue, the extract from Act One printed above follows the text of *Hamlet*. Rosencrantz and Guildenstern have been summoned to the king and here Claudius and Gertrude explain that their task is to find out why Hamlet is behaving so strangely; as Claudius puts it, to explain his 'transformation'. The lines then are from *Hamlet* but the way the audience experiences those lines in Stoppard's play is very different because of the framing and the context. Whereas in *Hamlet,* Rosencrantz and Guildenstern appear at this point as minor characters called to perform a specific function, in Stoppard's play the audience is focused more on their confusion and uncertainty. When the play opens they are passing the time tossing coins and recall that they have been summoned to the king but do not know why, 'An awakening, a man standing on his saddle to bang on the shutters, our names shouted in a certain dawn, a message, as summons . . .' Although the text in this extract is largely from *Hamlet,* the stage directions are Stoppard's. The confusion over names is a source of humour but the lack of clear identity which it conveys is also central to the author's intentions and the meaning of the play as a whole.

The confusion and powerlessness which Rosencrantz and Guildenstern experience, which is a major source of the ironic humour in the play and central to its meaning, occurs at different levels. Both in *Hamlet* and in *Rosencrantz and Guildenstern are Dead* the characters not only have little knowledge of what is going on but they are also subject to the whim of those more powerful than themselves. Rosencrantz draws attention to this fact in the extract:

> Both your majesties
> Might, by the sovereign power you have of us,
> Put your dread pleasures more into command
> Than to entreaty.

In Stoppard's play their confusion goes further because its source is deeper – they are characters in a play but they do not know that they are. This strange paradox can best be conveyed by describing an approach Stoppard could have taken if his artistic intentions were completely different. He could have taken the characters of Rosencrantz and Guildenstern and fleshed out their existence in Elsinore, how they got to know Hamlet, where they live, what their relationship was like and so on. Stoppard's characters have no present, past or future because they are only defined in relation to the play. The distinction between the two possible approaches is worth making because it is in the former sense that a drama teacher is likely to use 'minor characters' as a technique, but Stoppard's play gives an awareness of the full range of possibilities.

It is the second level of confusion which, for all its humorous content, gives the play its depth because Rosencrantz and Guildenstern are not only unable to understand what is going on around them, they are unable to make sense of their very existence. The tossing of the coins as a piece of framing action which extends into the first scene at the start of the play symbolises the arbitrary world which they inhabit. They have the feeling that they are within 'un-, sub- or supernatural forces.' As Guildenstern says, 'Wheels have been set in motion, and they have their own pace, to which we are . . . condemned.'

Thus in Stoppard's play the characters use a contemporary style of speech when they are operating outside the text of *Hamlet* as in the last line of the extract, 'I want to go home.' Their fragmented, panicked utterances when they hear of the task ahead of them also summarise the way they experience being in the world,

> ROS: I'm out of my step here –
> GUIL: We'll soon be home and high – dry and home – I'll –
> ROS: It's all over my *depth* –

Examples

It would be difficult for pupils to replicate the subtlety and complexity of Stoppard's play but the simple technique of seeing events through the eyes of minor characters presents many dramatic possibilities. 'Minor' in this case refers to the characters in relation to the main narrative, rather than in relation to the new drama which is created. Thus Rosencrantz and Guildenstern are the minor characters of *Hamlet* but become the main characters in Stoppard's play. The technique embodies characteristics of drama as art as described in the Introduction. It works obliquely in that it moves away from the central characters to provide a different, fresh perspective on the action. This in turn provides an element of distancing. Because that perspective will often be deliberately narrower (the point of view of the man who sold the gunpowder in a drama about Guy Fawkes is likely to be restricted) it operates through a process of constraint. The participants have to use the knowledge which they possess about an event in order to create a situation in which what they know is deliberately limited, thus providing opportunities for irony.

A more straightforward use of minor characters than in Stoppard's approach occurs in the *York Crucifixion Play*. Here the focus is on the soldiers erecting the cross. The dramatic effect lies in the contrast between the very narrow perspective and preoccupations of the soldiers compared with the awareness of the audience of the true significance of events.

> 2nd SOLDIER: I've got 'is 'ands, see – I'm not shirking!
> 3rd SOLDIER: I'll drag 'em to the 'ole we've bored –
> I don't think we'll need ropes and cord.

1st SOLDIER: Well, pull yer 'ardest, then by Jeez!
2nd SOLDIER: 'Ere is a good and solid pin –
                This nail should 'old 'is weight with ease.
                We'll stick it right through bone and skin
                No trouble – this job is a breeze!

O'Toole and Haseman (1987: 40) use the convention underlying the York play of changing the dramatic frame to create another drama project. The focus of the drama was the famous confrontation in an Olympic final between Zola Budd (a South African running for Britain) and Mary Decker (of the United States). After a number of activities involving the main characters, the actual event of the race itself is seen from the perspective of different 'minor' groups: Budd's family and friends in South Africa, sections of the crowd in the stadium including patriotic Americans, and neutrals watching on television. The dramatic frame is changed but the tension derived from the main action remains central.

The use of teacher in role can be rendered more effective by occupying a minor rather than central role. Thus, instead of becoming the mayor in a play about the Pied Piper, the role of clerk or secretary to the mayor may allow the teacher to have a foot in both camps. Heathcote, the founder and most famous exponent of this technique, often used an outsider role in relation to the drama, 'typically a very non-aggressive person from outside the community who wants to find out how they do things: the reporter who is getting facts for a story; the person in authority who needs to know what this group has been doing; the messenger who must make a report to the king; or the television or radio interviewer' (Wagner, 1976: 132). Woolland (1993: 58) identifies the advantages of what he describes as a 'second in command' role which can defer to a higher authority because it allows the teacher to seek assistance, bring information or transfer responsibility to the children.

Like many of the chapter titles in this book, the concept of 'minor characters' is less a 'technique' than a whole way of approaching drama. This can be illustrated by the thinking which underpins the 'mantle of the expert' approach also pioneered by Dorothy Heathcote. It has affinities with the notion of 'minor characters' in that it takes an oblique approach to its subject matter. In one series of lessons Heathcote was asked to base the drama on the legend of King Arthur. The approach she adopted was to put the pupils in role as beekeepers. That lateral leap, stated so baldly, may seem to border on the eccentric but the rationale is explained very clearly and convincingly in *Drama for Learning*. Although it is not possible to summarise the lesson here, some idea of the way it was approached can be gleaned from the way it was introduced. After some preliminary activities the theme was introduced by pinning a notice on the board:

> *"The British Broadcasting Company is anxious to meet experienced beekeepers who would assist in a living experiment regarding how bees were kept in the Dark Ages at the time when Arthur, High King of Britain, is thought to have reigned and brought peace to the kingdom. If you are interested, a representative from London will be glad to visit your group in order to explain the experiment in detail. "*
> (Heathcote and Bolton, 1995)

What is central to this notice and to the mantle of the expert approach is the way the pupils are given a functional role and endowed with an area of expertise. From the point of view of this chapter, the interesting dimension is the way in which the 'minor characters' are distanced through time and frame from the original subject matter ('King Arthur') in order paradoxically to bring them closer to it. Fines and Verrier (1974: 52) describe a drama approach to a topic on John Pym and Charles I in which the focus was not on the king but on how ordinary people might react to the arrival on their doorstep of a fugitive from royal justice. Drama based on the crusades explored different ways in which a young man who wanted to go off to fight in the crusades might deal with the problem of having to leave his widowed mother.

Approaching an event through the perspective of minor characters does not have to be confined to fictional or historical contexts but these have the advantage that the main events are already given, as for example when the events of the nativity play are seen from the point of view of the residents of Nazareth. A drama about Goldilocks and the Three Bears could begin with a questioning in role of Goldilock's neighbours to establish what they think of her. The approach, however, does not have to be confined to a situation in which the main events are given; these could evolve as part of the construction of the drama as in the following examples:

- The events of a wedding at which there is considerable friction between the two families could be seen through the perspective of the waiters, incorporating off-stage action (see Chapter 18).
- A football riot could be examined from the perspective of the manufacturers of the crash barriers. This has the potential for a mantle of the expert approach. In taking an oblique approach to a subject like this, care needs to be taken not to thwart the expectation of the pupils, but the excitement which the subject matter initially arouses could well be replaced by a deeper and more subtle set of tensions.

CHAPTER FIFTEEN

Monologue

I'd just taken her tea up this morning when she said, 'Graham, I think the world of you.' I said, 'I think the world of you.' And she said, 'That's all right then.' I said, 'What's brought this on?' She said, 'Nothing. This tea looks strong, pull the curtains.' Of course I knew what had brought it on. She said, 'I wouldn't like you to think you're not Number One.' So I said, 'Well, you're Number One with me too. Give me your teeth. I'll swill them.'

What it was we'd had a spot of excitement yesterday: we ran into a bit of Mother's past. I said to her, 'I didn't know you had a past. I thought I was your past.' She said, 'You?' I said, 'Well we go back a long way. How does he fit in vis-à-vis Dad?' She laughed. 'Oh, he was pre-Dad.' I said, 'Pre-Dad? I'm surprised you remember him, you don't remember to switch your blanket off.' She said, 'That's different. His name's Turnbull.' I said, 'I know. He said.'

I'd parked her by the war memorial on her usual seat while I went and got some reading matter. Then I waited while she went and spent a penny in the disabled toilet. She's not actually disabled, her memory's bad, but she says she prefers their toilets because you get more elbow room. She always takes for ever, diddling her hands and what not, and when she eventually comes back it turns out she's been chatting to the attendant. I said, 'What about?' She said, 'Hanging. She was in favour of stiffer penalties for minor offences and I thought, "Well, we know better, our Graham and me." I wish you'd been there, love; you could have given her the statistics, where are we going for our tea?'

The thing about Mam is that though she's never had a proper education, she's picked up enough from me to be able to hold her own in discussions about up-to-the-minute issues like the environment and the colour problem, and for a woman of her age and background she has a very liberal slant. She'll look at my *Guardian* and she actually thinks for herself. Doctor Chaudhury said to me, 'Full marks, Graham. The best way to avoid a broken hip is to have a flexible mind. Keep up the good work.'

They go mad round the war memorial so when we cross over I'll generally slip my arm through hers until we're safely across, only once we're on the pavement she'll postpone letting it go, because once upon a time we got stopped by one of these questionnaire women who reckons to take us for husband and wife. I mean, Mam's got white hair. She was doing this dodge and I said, 'Mam, let go of my arm.' I didn't really wrench it, only next thing I knew she's flat on the pavement. I said, 'Oh my God, Mother.'

Alan Bennett, A Chip in the Sugar

Commentary

This extract is the opening of the first of Alan Bennett's 'Talking Heads', a series of plays consisting entirely of monologues. The fact that one character addresses the audience for the entire performance raises interesting questions about the nature of the communication. Because there is only one speaker and no exchange between characters on stage, the form of communication with the audience is narrowed. For the monologue to have depth, therefore, irony and sub-text become important ingredients.

In *A Chip in the Sugar* the main speaker is Graham, a middle-aged man who still lives with his mother. We are given very little contextual information other than that the play is set in his bedroom, 'a small room with one window and one door. It is furnished with a single bed, a wardrobe, two chairs and nothing much else'. As the play proceeds the significance of the sparse bedroom becomes clear – Graham has little identity which is independent from his mother. The information we receive about their relationship is conveyed entirely by Graham himself as he relates the narrative of his 72-year-old mother's brief fling with one of her old flames, Mr Turnbull. We learn later in the play that the mother and Turnbull plan marriage but it turns out he already has a wife.

This extract embodies many of the features found in the monologue as a whole. For example, the use of reported direct speech is a way of making the presence of the other characters felt vividly although they are always represented and reported by Graham. The physical details ('give me your teeth') are a source of humour but also indicate the intimacy between them. The *non sequiturs* which combine the serious with the banal (the shift from talk about capital punishment to the question 'where are we going for tea?') are also a source of humour but indicative of the tone of the play as a whole which combines comedy and pathos.

Graham's intimate knowledge of his mother's domestic habits, her likes and dislikes, the portrayal of his disapproval and jealousy (a bit of mother's past) are all hinted at in this extract. The pathos which characterises the play as a whole can also be seen when Graham says that the woman 'reckons to take us for husband and wife'. The comment highlights the absence of any other relationship in Graham's life and draws attention to the way he has aged.

The key feature of Alan Bennett's monologues is the way the characters betray more than they realise (a form of dramatic irony). We see the events and characters solely through Graham's eyes and this narrowing of perspective is an inevitable ingredient of the dramatic form adopted. However, despite the narrowing of vision, his speech reveals more about his relationship with his mother than he realises. The account the audience is given is extremely subjective and this is brought home more clearly by the fact that only one person is speaking throughout. As the author himself has written, "None of these narrators after all is telling the whole story . . . Mr Turnbull may not be quite the common fellow ('could have been a bookie') the jealous Graham is ready to disparage" (Bennett, 1988: 7). Paradoxically, the narrowing of the perception is so clear it alerts the audience to wider potential meanings; inferences have to be made about the actual truth. It is Graham's jealousy of Mr Turnbull and the sadness of his own life which come across strongly in the monologue. The phrase 'a spot of excitement' works at two levels – Graham is intentionally ironic but the words betray the banality of his own existence. His jealousy is revealed in the phrase, 'I thought I was your past'.

The language carries more meaning than is at first apparent. 'I think the world of you' appears to be an expression of genuine affection, but we learn that what it has been brought on by are the events of the day before and the mother's awareness of Graham's jealousy. She takes his service totally for granted and her mild complaint about the strength of the tea is typical. Each utterance can carry several layers of meaning.

The dramatic tension needs to be embodied in the utterances of one character. In some ways monologue defies the rules of drama in that what we are getting is reported narrative rather than the concrete action in the 'here and now'. However because Graham himself is giving us insights into his life which he is only barely aware of himself, the tension derives from the subtle revelation of truth about the nature of his life and his relationship with his mother. There is no moralising because his relationship is not bitter; there is no strong sense that things should have been other.

It is appropriate to say, then, that the speaker betrays rather than articulates a state of mind. The audience is conscious of the author at work revealing meanings beyond the overt intention of the speaker. Another way of expressing this is that, although there is literally only one voice on stage, the drama itself expresses several voices. Although the basic technique is non-naturalistic, the drama follows naturalistic conventions within that broad device – the manner and content of Graham's speech is highly naturalistic.

In addition to dramatic monologues or monodramas which constitute the entire play, the term 'monologue' is often used within dramas whenever a character has an extended speech. Whether these are called monologues depends on whether *situational* or *structural* criteria are being used (Pfister, 1988: 127). In the first case the determining factor will be whether the speaker is alone on the stage at the time of speaking (as in the case of the soliloquy). The structural criterion refers to the length or degree of autonomy of a particular speech. Thus a publication such as Hooks (1994), *The Ultimate Scene and Monologue Sourcebook*, contains examples of speeches from plays which are often components of mdialogues. In this chapter I am confining the term 'monologue' to refer to moments when a dramatic figure is alone.

Study of monologues can help pupils understand how different points of view can be revealed in drama via sub-text, even though the utterances are limited to one person. Monologues tend to be written largely because it is very challenging to improvise a complete script. In the drama lesson they can be used as activities in their own right or as a means of giving depth to characterisation during the creation of a play.

Examples

How can monologues be used in drama teaching?
- pupils can be asked to work on the text of a monologue
- pupils can be asked to create their own monologues
- monologues can be used within drama for specific purposes
- monologues can be used as a way of framing dramatic action

As a way into Bennett's monologue, participants can be asked to focus on four lines of script represented as dialogue and experiment with reading them and creating a context.

A. Graham, I think the world of you.
B. I think the world of you.
A. That's all right then.
B. What's brought this on?
A. Nothing.

They could then try repeating the scene with the addition of the line, 'This tea looks strong, pull the curtains.' How does that single line change the likely context and meaning? How does this change the way the line is read? What happens if the lines are all delivered by one actor in a monologue? Does the actor differentiate between the words of the mother and his own words in the direct speech? What perspective would we get if the monologue was being delivered by the mother?

In improvised/process drama the monologue tends to be used less frequently because it tends not to lend itself to improvised work; it needs to be more deliberately constructed. Scripting and delivering monologues at the present time are more likely to be part of an examination syllabus. However working with monologues has considerable value because it draws attention very graphically to the way meaning works at different levels in drama. The following activities are designed to illustrate the way in which the words may communicate more than the speaker intends. The situations in the left column could be used for the creation of fairly straightforward monologues (see Goodwin and Taylor's *Solo* series for other examples). A far more demanding task, however, is to try to convey more subtle meanings. The greater the level of contrast between the overt and actual communication, the easier it is to grasp conceptually, but that in turn makes it more difficult to convey in the dialogue.

Situation	Overt communication	Actual communication	Typical lines
New teacher clearing away after a lesson talks about her experiences.	How she is succeeding at her job and enjoying it.	Things are not really going well.	The tenth years like to play the odd joke on me but that's all part of the fun of being in the school.
Teenager packing her case to leave home.	It is all her parents' fault.	She has been unreasonable.	If they wanted me to phone about staying out all night they should have said.

Situation	Overt communication	Actual communication	Typical lines
Prisoner in a cell reflecting on the events which got him there.	He is glad his friends were not caught.	He was left by his friends to take the punishment.	When they ran off like that I thought they were playing a joke because they never said anything.
Old person in a home.	She is delighted to be there and is glad that her children finally came to that decision.	She feels lonely and neglected.	Mary finds it hard to get in but I know they all think of me – I think they might be able to visit this Christmas.

Monologues may also be incorporated into improvised drama in order to summarise action, to reflect on action which has taken place (as when a captain keeps a log which records the experiences on board ship), or to create expectations about future action. Monologues of this kind can also be described as forms of narration and will be discussed more fully in Chapter 16.

A form of written monologue can be used to initiate the drama. For example, a pupil who is being bullied keeps a diary or writes a letter home; a worker writes a letter of resignation to his boss. Monologues can also be usefully employed at the start of an improvised drama to provide one character's perspective on the events which follow, e.g. a Year Nine class prepared sketches to demonstrate the problems encountered by a foreign visitor to an English family – each sketch began with the perspective of the visitor. This represents a form of counterpoint (see Chapter 4).

CHAPTER SIXTEEN

Narration

Enter MARGARET *with a cup which she takes to* MORE.

ALICE: Norfolk was speaking for you as Chancellor before he left.

MORE: He's a dangerous friend then. Wolsey's Chancellor, God help him. We don't want another. (MARGARET *takes cup to him; he sniffs it.*) I don't want this.

ALICE: Drink it. Great men get colds in the head just the same as commoners.

MORE: That's dangerous, levelling talk, Alice. Beware of the Tower. (*Rises.*) I will, I'll drink it in bed.

All move to stairs and ascend, talking.

MARGARET: Would you want to be Chancellor?

MORE: No.

MARGARET: That's what I said. But Norfolk said if Wolsey fell –

MORE (*no longer flippant*): If Wolsey fell, the splash would swamp a few small boats like ours. There will be no new Chancellors while Wolsey lives.

Exit above.

The light is dimmed there and a bright spot descends below. Into this bright circle from the wings is thrown the great red robe and the Cardinal's hat. The COMMON MAN *enters from the opposite wing and roughly piles them into his basket. He then takes from his pocket a pair of spectacles and from the basket a book. He reads:*

COMMON MAN (*reading*): 'Whether we follow tradition in ascribing Wolsey's death to a broken heart, or accept Professor Larcomb's less feeling diagnosis of pulmonary pneumonia, its effective cause was the King's displeasure. He died at Leicester on 29 November 1530 while on his way to the Tower under charge of High Treason.

'England's next Lord Chancellor was Sir Thomas More, a scholar and, by popular repute, a saint. His scholarship is supported by his writings; saintliness is a quality less easy to establish. But from his wilful indifference to realities which were obvious to quite ordinary contemporaries, it seems all too probable that he had it.'

Exit COMMON MAN. *As he goes, lights come up and a screen is lowered depicting Hampton Court.* CROMWELL *is sitting half-way up the stairs.*

Enter RICH, *crossing.*

CROMWELL: Rich! (RICH *stops, sees him, and smiles willingly.*) What brings you to Hampton?

RICH: I came with the Duke last night, Master Cromwell. They're hunting again.

CROMWELL: It's a kingly pastime, Master Rich. (*Both smile.*) I'm glad you found employment. You're the Duke's Secretary are you not?

RICH (*flustered*): My work *is* mostly secretarial.

CROMWELL (*as one making an effort of memory*): Or is it his librarian you are?

RICH: I do look after His Grace's library, yes.

CROMWELL: Oh. Well, that's something. And I don't suppose you're bothered much by His Grace – in the library? (RICH *smiles uncertainly.*) It's odd how differently men's fortunes flow. My late master died in disgrace, and here I am in the King's own service. There you are in a *comparative* back-water – yet the new Lord Chancellor's an old friend of yours.

Robert Bolt, *A Man for all Seasons*

Commentary

In the course of this short extract from Act One, the fall and death of Wolsey and the appointment of Thomas More as Lord Chancellor are summarised for the audience. Bolt's central interest in the play was More's refusal to save himself from death by swearing to the Act of Succession. Prior to those events, the death of Cardinal Wolsey and More's appointment as Lord Chancellor were important aspects of the historical development but their detailed exploration in the drama was not essential to Bolt's purpose.

The use of a narrator to describe aspects of the action was an ingredient of medieval drama. It was also common in plays written explicitly for performance in schools before the change in emphasis to dramatic playing in the 1950s. Both are examples of narration as a fairly crude device serving simply to summarise the plot or introduce the relevant characters. Bolt's purpose is, however, rather different. He could have used an alternative technique to convey the necessary information. As we see in this extract, the information about Rich's appointment is conveyed easily enough in the course of the dialogue. When we first meet him in the opening scene he is looking for employment – here the interim development is summarised in the exchange with Cromwell. Similarly Cromwell's own present position emerges in the natural flow of the conversation, 'My late master died in disgrace, and here I am in the King's own service.' Bolt then could have employed dialogue to summarise the death of Wolsey. However, his use of narration in this scene is part of the alienation device which is used throughout the play – it thus serves both a functional and an aesthetic role. This is enhanced by the symbolic way in which the fall of the Cardinal is depicted – the great red robe and Cardinal's hat are thrown into a spotlight symbolising his death.

The Common Man takes a number of different roles: as servant, steward, jailer, and jury foreman within the play. He is deliberately given no specific identity and he stage-manages the action, producing necessary props from a basket. The effect of these Brechtian techniques is to draw attention to the play's theatricality and illusion. For example, for More's trial the jury are represented as hats. It is in this context that the narration of the Common Man needs to be seen. Bolt's intention was to 'draw the audience into the play, not thrust them off it' (Bolt, 1960: xviii). He argued that the proper effect of alienation on the audience is 'to deepen, not to terminate, their involvement in the play' (ibid.: xvii).

A narrator who is also one of the characters is used in Miller's *A View From the Bridge*. Here the lawyer who plays a relatively minor role in the drama gives a perspective on the action at various points in the play. The role is similar to that of narrator, but there are crucial differences. If it is a specific dramatic figure in the play who is speaking (unlike the Common Man who does not correspond to one character alone), the perspective is inevitably restricted. When examining the use of narration in the creation of drama, it is useful to consider its use both from within and from outside the action of the play.

Examples

Judging by the literature of the time, narration tended to be used more widely in the educational drama of the 1970s because of the greater reliance on narrative progression and continuity. A popular contemporary approach is to use montage which does not demand the complete recounting of a plot. Typically the drama operates by working through a number of conventions like tableaux and hot-seating in an episodic way which, if operated too mechanistically, might deny pupils a sense of developing story/ plot. The use of narration can help in the process of creating drama but, as will be described below, it has its own risks. Narration in drama is generally recognised as fulfilling a number of functions. It can be used:

- to summarise action which would otherwise be difficult to enact
- to create an appropriate mood
- to initiate drama
- to bring drama to a close
- to inject extra elements of tension
- to give unity to work which would otherwise be fragmented
- to introduce teacher in role.

Summarising action

O'Neill (1995: 139) warns against too much reliance on narration which 'may reveal an incompetence or uncertainty in dealing with the material, a need to control or limit the response of the audience or participants, or it may expose the unsuitability of the material for dramatic purposes.' Morgan and Saxton (1987: 143) also draw attention to a potential problem, 'narration is a technique which must not be over-used or be so long that it becomes the teacher's story and not the pupils'.' These are appropriate warnings because there is a danger that narration, whether used by the teacher or by the pupils, will serve to side-step all the interesting challenges which the creation of dramatic *action* poses.

However, provided the dramatic focus of the action is clear, the use of narration can summarise events which might otherwise be difficult to depict and which are not of central interest to the plot. Both considerations should be borne in mind. It is usually possible to find an effective means of depicting any kind of event in drama (tableaux, mime, movement, dance drama) but it may be more appropriate, in particular contexts, to narrate them. In a play about a shipwreck which has as its main focus the establishment of responsibility for what happened, the actual events of the shipwreck itself could be narrated because they are of less interest to the dramatic plot. This narration could take place outside the drama or could be integrated into the action as the survivors recount what happened to a committee of enquiry.

Similarly, in the following example based on an expedition (Kempe, 1996: 42), the teacher wanted to move the class on to a different situation in which their preparations would be tested, so the interim action could be summarised,

> The journey into the jungle took seven days. They paddled upstream in their canoes. It was the hardest week of the explorers' lives. They managed to escape from an attack by crocodiles and only narrowly survived when they had to paddle through some terrifying rapids . . .

Creating mood

The use of narration in Bolt's play has an aesthetic as well as functional role. In the following example, Neelands (1990: 53) describes a use of narration which has a number of purposes, but one of the most significant here is the way it helps to create mood:

> A group of scientists are preparing to investigate a UFO that has landed in a remote place. As they walk slowly towards the object, the teacher uses narration to slow down the pace, create the atmosphere of the moment, suggest the scientists' attitudes and expectations, build tension and belief into the context.

The narrative has a distancing effect but that does not mean reduction in commitment to the make-believe. It is the deliberate recognition of the events as fiction which 'draws the participants in', to adapt Bolt's phrase.

Initiating drama

Davies (1983: 31) describes a way of using narrative in order to initiate drama. What is important to notice is, in contrast to the previous example, the absence of any attempt to create a particular mood. The account is deliberately low key and matter-of-fact because the children have to have time to become involved and gain ownership of the work:

> I was running though a forest one day, when suddenly I tripped and fell. I looked to see what had caused me to trip, and I discovered a metal ring fixed to the ground. I wondered what it was doing in the middle of the forest, but I had not time to find out just then, but I was determined to return, and bring some helpers with me. Will you come with me and find out what it means?

Too much animation and excitement by the teacher in the early stages of the drama would simply not ring true for the pupils.

Here is an example of the way Heathcote (Heathcote and Bolton, 1995: 88) initiates a drama. She uses a style of musing and questioning rather than narrative as such, but her opening sentence is full of relevant narrative information:

> They say that scientists who try to find out about what makes people ill get their money from the government in Washington, and the President signs the checks.

Bringing drama to a close

In a drama based on the Biblical story of Joseph and his Brothers, Bolton (1992: 92) used narration which both described and directed the action to bring the work to a close. As he spoke, the ten/eleven year olds in role as Joseph's brothers pushed the teacher (in role as Joseph) into the pit:

> And they watched their brother disappear into the blackness of the pit . . . until they could hardly see him at all . . . and then . . . when they realised what they had done, they moved backwards, as one body, from the edge of the pit . . . [now the narrating has turned to explicit instructing] they turned round, picked up their gear and, with one of them carrying the boy's coat, they walked in the direction of home, knowing that they had to find a way to tell their father that his favourite son was dead.

The example illustrates very clearly that narration does not have to be a substitute for action.

Injecting tension

Teacher narrative may serve to inject tension which was not apparent up to that point in the play. The narrative here is not outside the drama but takes the form of a monologue delivered by one of the characters. 'Tonight we made camp at the edge of the forest. I am beginning to realise that some people are not happy with the decisions I have taken. I know that I am likely to face similar problems tomorrow. Some of them think that my idea to risk the short cut through the forest is too dangerous . . .' The purpose of the monologue is to summarise what has happened so far, and to give pointers to the way the drama could develop.

Unifying work

Young pupils took the part of villagers in another example in which much of the initial work took place in small groups. A sense of unity can be given to the fragmented action by teacher narration which summarises the events of the day in the life of the village and sets the scene for what is to follow. Similarly a drama about a person's life story in which different groups enact a selection of moments in the individual's life can be brought together by teacher narration.

Introducing teacher in role

Bolton (1992: 73), in a drama based on Robin Hood, describes to the participants how he plans to use narration to introduce teacher in role:

Let us assume that it is noon on a hot summer's day, so that you are either working outside your houses or at least with all windows and doors thrown open. Then it will be easy for you to see a stranger arriving: first the sound of horse's hoofs and then, when he appears, you will see from his apparel that he is one of Robin Hood's men. I shall play the stranger but, instead of suddenly appearing, I shall start to 'narrate' his entrance. I shall say something like: 'Absorbed in their task they were surprised to realise they had a visitor . . . .They did not know him, but recognised . . .' and so on. I will start interacting with you.

This is an interesting and subtle example which illustrates that narration is used best when it is not merely functional. When the teacher actually begins the narration, it is not to provide them with information because this has already been achieved by introductory comments. The narration is rather part of the drama itself, setting the appropriate mood and atmosphere.

Most of the above examples are taken from teacher-led drama projects but, as with other conventions and techniques in this book, the device can equally be used in pupils' own play-making. The point, however, is that narration, when appropriately used, is not a substitute for dramatic action but is incorporated into the dramatic structure and used for specific purposes.

CHAPTER SEVENTEEN

Object Focus

MARLOW: (*Aside to* WHEELER) Have you seen the cigarette-box?

WHEELER: No.

MARLOW: Well, it's gone. I put it on the tray last night. And he's been smoking. (*Showing her the ends of cigarette.*) It's not in these pockets. He can't have taken it upstairs this morning! Have a good look in his room when he comes down. Who's been in here?

WHEELER: Only me and Mrs Jones.

MRS JONES: I've finished here; shall I do the drawing-room now?

WHEELER: (*Looking at her doubtfully*) Have you seen— Best do the boudwower first.

(MRS JONES *goes out with pan and brush.* MARLOW *and* WHEELER *look each other in the face.*)

MARLOW: It'll turn up.

WHEELER: (*Hesitating*) You don't think she— (*Nodding at the door.*)

MARLOW: (*Stoutly.*) I don't – I never believes anything of anybody.

WHEELER: But the master'll have to be told.

MARLOW: You wait a bit, and see if it don't turn up. Suspicion's no business of ours. I set my mind against it.

John Galsworthy, The Silver Box

*   *   *

LORD WINDERMERE: Your carriage has not come back yet, Mrs. Erlynne.

MRS ERLYNNE: It makes no matter. I'll take a hansom. There is nothing in the world so respectable as a good Shrewsbury and Talbot. And now, dear Lady Windermere, I am afraid it is really good-bye. (*Moves up C.*) Oh, I remember. You'll think me absurd, but do you know I've taken a great fancy to this fan that I was silly enough to run away with last night from your ball. Now, I wonder would you give it to me? Lord Windermere says you may. I know it is his present.

LADY WINDERMERE: Oh, certainly, if it will give you any pleasure. But is has my name on it. It has 'Margaret' on it.

MRS ERLYNNE: But we have the same Christian name.

LADY WINDERMERE: Oh, I forgot. Of course, do have it. What a wonderful chance our names being the same!

MRS ERLYNNE: Quite wonderful. Thanks – it will always remind me of you. (*Shakes hands with her.*)

Oscar Wilde, Lady Windermere's Fan

*   *   *

OTHELLO: Is 't lost? Is 't gone? speak, is it out o' the way?

DESDEMONA: Heaven bless us!

OTHELLO: Say you?

DESDEMONA: It is not lost, but what an if it were?

OTHELLO: Ha!

DESDEMONA: I say it is not lost.

OTHELLO: Fetch 't, let me see it.

DESDEMONA: Why, so I can, sir, but I will not now,
This is a trick to put me from my suit,
I pray let Cassio be receiv'd again.

OTHELLO: Fetch me that handkerchief, my mind misgives.

DESDEMONA: Come, come,
You'll never meet a more sufficient man.

OTHELLO: The handkerchief!

DESDEMONA: I pray, talk me of Cassio.

OTHELLO: The handkerchief!

William Shakespeare, Othello

Commentary

The action of the drama in each of the extracts from the three plays centres on specific objects: a silver cigarette case which is stolen, a lady's fan and a handkerchief. In the first two examples, the object in question is also the title of the play, signalling the importance the author attached to it. In each case the objects provide a focus and anchor for the dramatic structure.

In *The Silver Box* the action centres on the cigarette case throughout the play. In the first scene Jack, the upper-class son who, while drunk, has stolen a girl's purse, is helped home by Jones, the unemployed worker. When Jack falls asleep, Jones steals the cigarette box. The extract above is taken from Scene Two when the fact that the cigarette box is missing is discovered by butler and servant. Suspicion inevitably falls on Mrs Jones who cleans for the family, but she in turn discovers that her husband is the guilty party. The two men are treated differently despite the similarities of their crimes and motivation (they both act out of spite). The father is able to protect his son because of his wealth; Jones is sent to prison.

It is a very straightforward play, first performed in 1906 and very much of its time, with its extremely conventional structure, neat plot, topical detail and slightly archaic language. The silver box appears in every scene giving unity to the action. The box is not intended to be seen symbolically in this highly naturalistic play, but it does accrue symbolic force because it comes to represent the wealth of the upper classes. The focus on a concrete object also helps to particularise the play and place its fairly direct moral message in a very specific context.

The second extract comes from near the end of Oscar Wilde's play. Mrs Erlynne is pleased to receive the fan as a gift because Lady Windermere, without realising it, is in fact her daughter. Once again the object knits the plot together. At the start of the play we discover that it is a present given to Lady Windermere by her husband. She, unaware of Mrs Erlynne's identity and suspicious that she is having a liaison with Lord Windermere, resolves to strike her with the fan if she comes to the house. In the third act the discovery of the fan in another man's house leads Lord Windermere to suspect his wife but he is distracted by Mrs Erlynne's quick thinking and intervention, 'I am afraid that I took your wife's fan in mistake for my own when I was leaving your house tonight'. Once again the object is central to the structure of the plot but it also accrues symbolic significance when it is given as a gift to the mother.

In Shakespeare's play the handkerchief is central to Iago's plot to manipulate Othello into thinking his wife has been unfaithful with Cassio. The extract (from Act 3 Scene 4) is particularly ironic. Othello is demanding to see the handkerchief because Iago has led him to believe that Desdemona has given it to Cassio. Desdemona's response is to distract him by pleading for Cassio. A rational mind would see that her actions are hardly those of someone who is guilty. The object takes on major significance because the sight of Cassio with his wife's handkerchief is the one concrete piece of evidence to which he can cling in order to confirm his suspicions. When he is about to murder Desdemona he makes reference to it,

> That handkerchief which I so loved and gave thee,
> Thou gav'st to Cassio.

And again when he has discovered her innocence, it is playing on his mind,

> How came you, Cassio, by that handkerchief
> That was my wife's?

The handkerchief is of great significance in the tragedy because it represents the 'ocular proof' Othello requires. It is endowed with enormous meaning because in his mind it comes to stand for her adultery. The handkerchief is something concrete for Othello to hold on to as final proof of his wife's infidelity.

In each of the plays concrete objects are used in slightly different ways but they all provide a focus for the dramatic structure and take on an element of symbolism.

Examples

The use of 'object focus' in drama refers to the use of one central concrete focus as in the examples given, as opposed to the use of props. It can serve a number of functions:

- as a starting point for the drama
- as a means of focusing the action
- as a device to help concentrate on plot rather than narrative
- as a means of introducing symbolism
- as a way of particularising the drama.

Objects are useful starting points for drama with young pupils. Davies (1983: 33) suggests that a number of questions to the children, such as 'Who could use this?' 'What could it be used for?' 'Where did you find it?' 'What does it mean?', may get the drama started in a way which does not restrict the pupils' choices unduly. Readman and Lamont (1994: 30) list the types of artefacts which can lead to dramas of mystery, secrecy and suspense: a half-written letter from someone requesting help in order to escape from a tyrant or dictator; a broken toy which is the only evidence of a runaway child's identity; or a St Christopher medal which everyone who crosses the dangerous cavern has to wear. Woolland (1993: 95) describes the way in which objects can take on symbolic significance; for example, an empty bowl can signify hunger and poverty or be a gift from a skilled craftsman. A number of the lessons described by Peter (1994) designed for pupils with special educational needs use concrete objects (a hat, a teddy, a bundle of clothes) as starting points. Cattanach (1992: 84) suggests that play with objects, making objects with clay can be a way to stimulate drama for people with physical disabilities.

Objects can be used as a starting point and focus for the drama when the children are framed as investigators. The following 'template' plan (with pupils aged ten or eleven in mind) can be adapted according to context. The precise shaping and construction of the drama will clearly depend on the pupils' responses and the choice of object. Central to the work, however, is the establishment of how the object came to be buried and what story it has to tell. Historical artefacts will clearly take the drama in one direction; other objects such as a piece of jewellery or a briefcase will more likely lead to drama about theft or murder.

1. Pupils are placed in role as historians, archaeologists or simply investigators. This could be achieved by discussion or in role, by asking them to talk about previous cases in which they have been involved. It is established that the drama will be based on the discovery of a particular object which can be shown to the pupils at this stage. The 'discovery' in the fiction does not have to be real. In fact a 'real' discovery within the drama might make belief in the fiction less rather than more likely.
2. The class is taken to the site where the discovery was made. In role they take measurements, photograph the site, make diagrams and drawings. This part of the lesson can be conducted in groups with the presence of the object being simply imagined in each. Notice that the presence of the physical object is not vital for enacting the drama once it has been established as the central focus of the fiction. Alternatively, the scene can be enacted as a form of forum theatre with one group of investigators being observed and directed by the others. In this case the real object can be used.
3. The pupils interview the person who made the discovery (teacher in role) to establish that this was not a hoax and to gather any extra useful information. Alternatively, this part of the lesson may be conducted in pairs but in that case some discussion needs to establish which information from the pairs' work feeds into the class drama.
4. The pupils report back to teacher in role as their supervisor about their thoughts and speculations. This may be a useful interim stage which establishes what still needs to be found out and can be followed by a repeat of the earlier stages.
5. They create tableaux showing a context in which the object might have been used. Alternatively they show a series of tableaux showing the varied history of the object over time.
6. The development of the next stage will depend on the experience of the pupils but they could be asked to enact one of the scenes, or they could prepare a brief television report about the discovery.

The following drama used teacher in role with a small group of special needs children in which the objects provided a clue to a homeless man's past life. As always with this type of extended teacher in role, it is helpful (although not essential) if there is someone else to lead the drama.

1. After some initial discussion the teacher invites the pupils to participate in a play about a homeless man who has lost his memory. The objects he has in his bag will give a clue to his identity. He tells them that he is going to be that person and they watch as he puts on an old torn coat and hat, dirties his face a little, places a plaster over one eye and clutches a carrier bag. There is no intention to deceive the pupils; they need to know that a fiction is being created. Some teachers prefer the impact of appearing in role rather than having the pupils watch the transformation. Either way, I think it is important for the pupils to see the teacher as teacher before the drama begins.

2. He adopts a stance of someone who is scared and ready to leave at a moment's notice. The first challenge for the pupils is to reassure him and persuade him to stay.

3. The drama here works through constraint. The goal is for the pupils to be able to see what is inside the bag, but it is for the teacher in role to make them work to gain his trust and persuade him to hand it over.

4. The bag contains objects which, through questioning, gradually help the man to regain his memory. Choice and number of objects will depend on the group but the following list indicates the variety of possibilities which have been used in the past in different combinations (a dice, a letter, a train ticket, a diary, a photograph, tools, bicycle clips, an old family Bible). The objects do not need to tell a complete story – they need only suggest a past which can be negotiated with teacher in role as the drama develops.

5. The final part of this sequence involving teacher in role may be the starting point for a drama based on what has been discovered, examining aspects of the man's life story.

Fines and Verrier (1974: 29) describe a lesson with a group of eleven/ twelve year olds whose topic was medieval villages. They decided that they would approach the topic by establishing a coroner's court of the period. It was essential to have an appropriate start, 'an object as evidence seemed most suitable: it could hold attention by its own interest, would act as a focus, and have what I have come to feel is hypnotic power – a single object, uncluttered by all else, reverently handled, unavoidable.' The object chosen was a museum replica of a carved amulet. The lesson took the form of high risk 'living though' drama but the focus on the object helped sustain belief and concentration. The teacher first established a contract with the class that if they formed a coroner's court and tried to believe in it he would make something happen. The teacher in role initiated the drama, establishing that the court had met to investigate a murder; the thief had taken everything which might identify the murder victim except the talisman. From that point on the drama developed from within by negotiation, with various accusations and counter-accusations.

In each of the lessons described, the objects chosen helped to sustain belief and concentration in the drama, gave unity to the plot and provided a concrete symbol related to the theme of the work.

CHAPTER EIGHTEEN
Off-Stage Action

[*Sidney and Jane Hopcroft's kitchen.*

Jane is in the kitchen and about to make an entrance into the living room where the guests have just arrived when she notices she is still wearing her bedroom slippers.]

JANE: Oh.

(*She takes off her slippers, puts them on the table and scuttles round the kitchen looking for her shoes. She cannot find them. She picks up the slippers and wipes the table with their fluffy side, where they have made a mark.*)

Oh.

(*She hurries back to the door, opens it a fraction. Jolly chatter and laughter is heard.* JANE *stands for a long time, peeping through the crack in the door, trying to catch sight of her shoes. She sees them. She closes the door again. She stands lost.*)

Oh. Oh. Oh.

(*The door opens. Loud laughter from off.* SIDNEY *comes in laughing. He closes the door. The laughter cuts off abruptly.*)

SIDNEY (*fiercely, in a low voice*): Come on. What are you doing?
JANE: I can't.
SIDNEY: What?
JANE: I've got no shoes.
SIDNEY: What do you mean, no shoes?
JANE: They're in there.
SIDNEY: Where?
JANE: By the fireplace. I left them so I could slip them on.

126

SIDNEY: Well, then, why didn't you?

JANE: I didn't have time. I forgot.

SIDNEY: Well, come and get them.

JANE: No . . .

SIDNEY: It's only Dick and Lottie Potter.

JANE: You fetch them.

SIDNEY: I can't fetch them.

JANE: Yes, you can. Pick them up and bring them in here.

SIDNEY: But I . . .

JANE: Sidney, please.

SIDNEY: Dear oh dear. What a start. I say, what a start. (*He opens the door cautiously and listens. Silence.*) They've stopped talking.

JANE: Have they?

SIDNEY: Wondering where we are, no doubt.

JANE: Well, go in. Here.

SIDNEY: What?

JANE: (*Handing him her slippers*): Take these.

SIDNEY: What do I do with these?

JANE: The hall cupboard.

SIDNEY: You're really expecting rather a lot tonight, aren't you?

JANE: I'm sorry.

SIDNEY: Yes, well it's got to stop. It's got to stop. I have to entertain out there, you know. (*He opens the door and starts laughing heartily as he does so.*)

(SIDNEY *goes out, closing the door.*)

(JANE *hurries about nervously, making still more adjustments to her person and checking her appearance in the mirror.*)

(*At length the door opens, letting in a bellow of laughter.* SIDNEY *returns, carrying* JANE's *shoes.*)

(*Behind him.*) Yes, I will. I will. I'll tell her that, Dick . . . (*He laughs until he's shut the door. His laugh cuts off abruptly. Thrusting* JANE's *shoes at her, ungraciously.*) Here.

JANE: Oh, thank goodness.

SIDNEY: Now for heavens sake, come in.

JANE: (*struggling into her shoes*): Yes, I'm sorry. What did Dick say?

SIDNEY: When?

JANE: Just now? That you told him you'd tell me.

SIDNEY: I really can't remember. Now then, are you ready?

JANE: Yes, yes.

SIDNEY: It's a good job it's only Dick and Lottie out there. It might have
been the Brewster-Wrights. I'd have had a job explaining this to them.
Walking in and out like a shoe salesman. All right?
JANE: Yes.
SIDNEY: Right. (*He throws open the door, jovially.*) Here she is. (*Pushing*
JANE *ahead of him*) Here she is at last.
(*Hearty cries of 'Ah ha' from* DICK *and* LOTTIE.)
JANE (*going in*): Here I am.

Alan Ayckbourn, Absurd Person Singular.

Commentary

This deceptively simple scene occurs near the beginning of Alan
Ayckbourn's comedy. Each act takes place on Christmas Eve in the kitchen
of one of the families' homes. The play exploits the technique of 'off-stage
action' for comic effect but also explores a central, more serious theme: the
contrast between public and private lives. The first act is focused on a party
which the Hopcrofts are holding in their home. Instead of placing the
action of the play in the living room where the party takes place, the author
situates it in the kitchen. We never actually see Lottie and Dick, although
we do meet the other guests as they enter and leave the kitchen for various
reasons.

Ayckbourn's first instinct was to set the action in the living room. He
explains his reason for changing to the kitchen in the Preface to the play:

> I was halfway through the act before I realised that I was viewing the
> evening from totally the wrong perspective. Dick and Lottie were
> indeed monstrously overwhelming, hearty and ultimately very bor-
> ing, and far better heard occasionally but not seen. By a simple device
> of switching to the kitchen, the problem was all but solved, adding
> incidentally far greater comic possibilities than the sitting room held.
> For in this particular case the off-stage action was far more relevant
> than its on-stage counterpart.

(Ayckbourn, 1977)

At one level the scene works as pure farce, focusing as it does on Jane's
obsession with getting her shoes back, but there is deeper social satire both
in the play as a whole and in this extract. In a very economical way the
author manages to show Sidney's snobbery and social climbing ('It's a
good job it's only Dick and Lottie out there. It might have been the
Brewster-Wrights . . . Walking in and out like a shoe salesman'); he hints

at the nature of the relationship between Jane and Sidney ('You're really expecting rather a lot tonight, aren't you?') and Jane's obsession with cleanliness and tidiness which are emphasised throughout the play (her cleaning of the table with the slippers and her concern to have them put away in the appropriate place). The framing action at the start (frantically cleaning and peeping through the door looking for her shoes) emphasises her nervousness. We are able to observe the private interaction between the Hopcrofts while their public selves which are retained for the visitors are left largely to our imagination. The falsity of the artificial and highly managed exchanges with the visitors does not need to be shown but merely hinted at by the abrupt way Sidney's manner changes when he moves from living room to kitchen. His insincerity and concern with the form rather than the substance of social interaction is revealed by his comment to his guest, 'Yes, I will. I will. I'll tell her that, Dick' and his reply when Jane asks him what he was supposed to tell her, 'I really can't remember'.

It is not too fanciful to view what is happening in this scene as a metaphor for drama itself. The Hopcrofts, particularly Sidney, are trying to 'manage' a social exchange. Bolton (1992) draws a parallel between the 'managing' or 'working at' social situations which occurs in real life and the process of engaging in dramatic playing activity. In the extract it is as if the Hopcrofts are waiting to go on-stage every time they enter the living room and present a role to the assembled guests. The gap between reality and the way they manage the presentation of their false selves is a central theme of the play which becomes more significant in a later scene when the wife of one of the guests is trying to commit suicide. They are so preoccupied with maintaining their roles that they fail to notice what she is up to.

The convention which is the subject of this chapter has close affinities to reported action (Chapter 21) but there is a key difference. In the case of reported action the audience is being told about events which have happened some time in the past – it therefore operates in narrative mode. With off-stage action, however, we are being asked to imagine that events are going on simultaneously and interacting with the overt focus of the on-stage action. The technique serves not so much to move the plot forward as to provide the action with more depth. This is a graphic, concrete manifestation of the way drama frequently works in that a particular utterance, exchange or action gains greater depth by hinting at what is *not* being presented, and another world is implied. The on-stage action necessarily relates to what is happening off-stage so there is an automatic focus: causality, reactions to events and the nature of relationships can all be explored by this oblique approach.

Examples

The simplicity of the dialogue in this extract makes it a useful one for introducing the convention to older pupils. They can be given the first twelve lines without the stage directions and asked to suggest a possible context. A plausible situation is fairly easy to create and most participants will quickly get the sense of what the context is likely to be. This preliminary exercise is a useful way of introducing the extract and can draw pupils' attention to the way information is conveyed in the lines very economically. The extract can then be performed while the scene in the living room is depicted as a still image. In order to make the off-stage action more concrete, the interactions in the living room can be conveyed by mime when one or other of the Hopcrofts enter.

Alternatively the opening lines can be used as a starting point for an improvisation which continues in the same vein, with the characters interacting and intermittently leaving to go to the other room. Another possible approach is to ask the pupils to enact the scene which takes place in the living room while the Hopcrofts are in the kitchen. In this activity pupils can be encouraged to highlight the contrast between the image Jane and Sidney have of themselves and the way they are seen by their guests.

Because the convention works by leaving the off-stage action to the imagination, it is a very clear example of an oblique approach to drama. As suggested above, it has affinities with reported action. Both techniques allow action which may be difficult to depict on-stage to happen off-stage, and both operate as distancing devices whereby scenes which may be too emotionally loaded can be approached indirectly. Sentimentality and embarrassment can thus be avoided. The fact that the drama demands a unity of place (in Ayckbourn's play the events happen in the kitchen) makes the structure more manageable.

There are however artistic as well as these pragmatic reasons for using the technique because it brings a different perspective on the chosen theme. The on-stage play has the potential to promote reflection on what is happening off-stage in a way which would not happen if the drama was caught up in depicting the actual events. However, it is a particular type of distancing because the events being referred to are happening in the present. Often the drama will concern itself with the way people react to the main events, thereby provoking more analysis. Just as participation in drama releases the spectator, the on-stage action reflects on what is happening off-stage.

Here then is a summary of practical considerations when using this convention:

- the on-stage activity interacts with events which are happening simultaneously off-stage;
- the action is created in the minds of the audience by what is said on-stage;
- the dramatic context needs to allow characters to come and go;
- it helps therefore if the off-stage events are in progress nearby;
- sometimes it is appropriate for the audience to hear a snippet of conversation;
- and have the characters interact briefly with those off-stage;
- the on-stage action is likely to be confined to one place.

The device can be used to create a drama in its own right or as a convention within an ongoing drama. The convention lends itself to comedy because it does tend to invite a contrast between private and public faces, pretence and reality but it can treat serious subjects as well. In the case of Ayckbourn's play the comedy has serious undertones.

Here are some examples employing off-stage action:

- A disco is seen from the perspective of the social gatherings which happen away from the main action. The relationships, rivalries, arguments can all be explored by the way people react in the privacy of the toilets. A group of pupils created a complicated scenario of jealousies and changing affiliations through the comings and goings in the toilets. They made the outside events seem more real by simple references such as, 'Oh, let's go, I like this record.'

  Russell uses a similar technique in *Stags and Hens* in which the action switches between the Ladies and Gents toilets. The opening of the play is set in a Liverpool dance hall but takes place in the Ladies. Linda, whose hen night the girls have come to celebrate, goes straight into a cubicle. The others start putting on their make-up.

  MAUREEN (*crying*): Congratulations Linda. Congratulations.
  BERNADETTE: What's up with you now?
  MAUREEN: I don't know.
  BERNADETTE: Cryin'! On a hen night! It's supposed to be a happy night.
  MAUREEN (*bawling*): I am happy. I'm very happy . . . for Linda.
  CAROL (*calling out to* LINDA): We're all happy for y' Linda. Ogh Lind, you lucky sod!

- The surprise visit of a Good Food Guide inspector to a restaurant or the problems dealing with a particularly fussy customer are explored through the reactions of the manager and staff in the kitchen. This situation lends itself to humorous treatment and is reminiscent of the television series *Fawlty Towers,* although in that case the camera switched between restaurant and kitchen. The panic 'back-stage' is well conveyed in the following extract in which Basil is trying to fulfil a customer's demand for a Waldorf salad.

BASIL: There's no celery, there's no grapes . . . walnuts! That's a laugh, easier to find a packet of sliced hippopotamus in suitcase sauce than a walnut in this bloody kitchen. (*he looks in the fridge*)

SYBIL: Now, we've got apples. (*holding up some*)

BASIL: Oh, terrific! Let's celebrate. We'll have an apple party. Everybody brings his own apple and stuffs it down somebody's throat.

SYBIL: Basil, I'll find everything. Just go and get a bottle of Volnay.

BASIL: What's a waldorf anyway – a walnut that's gone off?

- The escalation of a riot is seen from the perspective of the first-aid room. Notice that the aim here is not to show the aftermath (which could be another approach to the topic) but to show how events unfold. The scene can be given more depth by seeking to provide some extra insight into the events which is denied to those caught up in the main action. There might be an opportunity to bring together rival groups who come to see each other differently in the relative calm of the medical room.

- The tensions deriving from inter-personal relations involved in putting on a play are explored through what happens back-stage, with the actors making their entrances and exits. Pupils who created a short scene based on this scenario set the actors facing the audience as if sitting at a mirror and conducted the conversation as they prepared for their entrance.

- The turmoil of a busy hospital is shown from the perspective of the nurses' recreation room where they snatch short coffee breaks. Again the comings and goings can convey a number of complicated scenarios happening off-stage. The drama, for example, might explore difficult ethical decisions to do with whether to turn off a life support machine.

CHAPTER NINETEEN

Pause

Pub. 1977. Spring.

Noon.

EMMA *is sitting at a corner table.* JERRY *approaches with drinks, a pint of bitter for him, a glass of wine for her.*

He sits. They smile, toast each other silently, drink.

He sits back and looks at her.

JERRY: Well . . .
EMMA: How are you?
JERRY: All right.
EMMA: You look well.
JERRY: Well, I'm not all that well, really.
EMMA: Why? What's the matter?
JERRY: Hangover.

He raises his glass

Cheers.

He drinks.

How are you?
EMMA: I'm fine.

She looks round the bar, back at him.

Just like old times.
JERRY: Mmn. It's been a long time.
EMMA: Yes.

Pause

I thought of you the other day.
JERRY: Good God. Why?

She laughs.

JERRY: Why?
EMMA: Well, it's nice, sometimes, to think back. Isn't it?
JERRY: Absolutely.

Pause

How's everything?
EMMA: Oh, not too bad.

Pause

Do you know how long it is since we met?
JERRY: Well I came to that private view, when was it –?
EMMA: No, I don't mean that.
JERRY: Oh you mean alone?
EMMA: Yes
JERRY: Uuh . . .
EMMA: Two years.
JERRY: Yes, I thought it must be. Mmnn.

Pause

EMMA: Long time.
JERRY: Yes. It is.

Pause

Harold Pinter, *Betrayal*

Commentary

This opening extract from the first scene of *Betrayal* is punctuated by
pauses which are typical of Pinter's plays and of much modern dramatic
writing. As the scene develops the audience is given more clues which
confirm what no doubt has been suspected from very early on in the play,
that Jerry and Emma have had an affair some time in the past. Jerry's comment, 'You remember the form. I ask about your husband, you ask about
my wife' is followed moments later by his calling her 'Darling', followed
by the reply, 'Don't say that'. The dialogue continues to provide more
clues until the details are finally spelled out by Jerry later in the scene, '. . .
the only thing I really felt was irritation . . . that nobody gossiped about us
. . . I nearly said, now look, . . . she and I had an affair for seven years . . .'
By the time the audience receive that exposition of the background, all
that needs to be confirmed is the length of the affair, although this is the

first time it is overtly acknowledged. Why is it that the members of the audience almost certainly know what to expect before they receive that confirmation? First of all, the title of the play, *Betrayal,* is one of the framing devices which might contribute to the audience's reading of the scene. Secondly, there are clues in the dialogue; Emma and Jerry recollect how long it is since they have been alone. They also make comments such as 'Just like old times' and 'I thought of you the other day' which suggest a past relationship. However it is also the silences and pauses which contribute to the audience's reaction to the scene because it is primarily these which determine the tone of the exchange and the implication that there is a strong sub-text. The pauses draw attention to what is *not* said and help create the impression from very early on in the exchange of words that this is more than just a meeting of old friends.

Timing of utterances in stage dialogue is more often a matter for actors and director rather than the author. It is usually in rehearsal that decisions are made about the pace at which lines should be delivered. Of course the text will often dictate its own rhythms, as in the case of the extract from *Macbeth* printed below (p. 138). However the pauses in the extract from *Betrayal,* as elsewhere in Pinter's work, are central to the author's intention and the text's meaning. The lack of overt emotion and content in the dialogue is important both to this scene and to the structure of the play overall. What the audience is observing in this exchange is actually a result of events which are about to be witnessed in the play.

The use of a particular form of time shift (Chapter 23) means that the play begins at the end of the relationship and works back through different scenes over a period of years to when it first started. The final Scene Nine is set at the wedding reception of Emma and her husband. The interest in *what happens* between Emma and Jerry is partly replaced by concern with *how it happens,* the source of a different type of dramatic tension. There is also, however, more to learn about the set of relationships and the meaning of the title *Betrayal.* The rest of the play from this first scene gives substance to the strong sub-text which is sensed but not fully understood here. The pauses are essential in conveying that sense of sub-text.

What the audience learn as the play progresses is that betrayal is pervasive in the triangular relationship: the wife betrays her husband, one friend betrays another by committing adultery with his wife, the husband betrays his wife in turn by being unfaithful with someone else. We learn also that Emma has deceived her lover Jerry by concealing from him the fact that her husband had been told of the relationship four years earlier:

ROBERT: She didn't tell me last night.

JERRY: What do you mean?

Pause

I know about last night. She told me about it. You were up all night, weren't you?

ROBERT: That's correct.

JERRY: And she told you . . . last night . . . about her and me. Did she not?

ROBERT: No, she didn't. She didn't tell me about you and her last night. She told me about you and her four years ago.

Pause

So she didn't have to tell me again last night. Because I knew. And she knew I knew because she told me herself four years ago.

Silence

The silences and pauses which are indicated by the stage directions as well as the dotted lines in the text, convey the depth of feeling and shock which is all the more effective because of the restraint. Pfister (1988: 45) has drawn attention to the contrast between the use of periods of silence in classical dramas and the silence which occurs in modern plays. In the former the intention is more often than not to create a 'pregnant pause' in order to show tension, emphasise certain aspects of the dialogue or to allow time for the audience to react. He suggests that the silences that occur in modern plays, by contrast, often serve to focus attention on the impossibility of speech:

> Like simultaneous speech, the use of fairly lengthy pauses between individual utterances can hardly be said to be a recent innovation in modern drama. Nonetheless, it was modern drama that first began to employ it with such innovative consistency. Whether the pauses are situated within a speech or between speeches, or whether they are filled with mime and gesture or are left devoid of non-verbal communication – they always reflect some degree of disrupted communication, the monological imprisonment of a dramatic figure in the world of its own imagination, an inability to establish contact with others, or even linguistic impotence.

In many of Pinter's plays the characters give the impression that they are evading rather than engaging in communication. Similarly in the work of Beckett the language often seems to function in order to fill the void rather than to effect any meaningful interaction:

ESTRAGON: I was. (*Gestures towards his rags.*) Isn't that obvious.

Silence.

VLADIMIR: Where was I . . . How's your foot?
ESTRAGON: Swelling visibly.
VLADIMIR: Ah yes, the two thieves. Do you remember the story?
ESTRAGON: No.
VLADIMIR: Shall I tell it to you?
ESTRAGON: No.
VLADIMIR: It'll pass the time. (*Pause.*)

In Beckett's *All That Fall,* the intensity of the ending and the ambiguity about what exactly happened to the little child is emphasised by the pauses. 'It was a little child fell out of the carriage, Ma'am. (*Pause*) On to the line, Ma'am. (*Pause*) Under the wheels, Ma'am'. In the last act of Chekhov's *The Seagull,* the actor playing Konstantin is given the following direction. '*Over the next two minutes he silently tears up all his manuscripts and throws them under the desk, then opens the righthand door and goes out.*' The length of the silence is a prelude to the dramatic climax which follows.

Examples

The extract from *Betrayal* printed here can be used with older pupils to provide a focus for the exploration of sub-text and pauses as in the following activities.

- Ask the pupils to read/enact the scene in two different ways, the second time with much more pace. For the second version the stage directions need to be changed but it may also be helpful to change the setting from a pub (and alter some of the lines accordingly). For example, one or both characters could be busy performing some action which makes the stillness and silences less likely than if they are simply sitting down opposite each other. The change in pace will alter the meaning of the dialogue in subtle ways.
- The pupils could create a contrasting scene which shows the two characters in the same pub years earlier. The silences and pauses would almost certainly be less in evidence because the weight of the intervening years and events will not be there.
- Ask one pair to read the dialogue while two others insert the sub-text at various points in the form of inner thoughts. This exercise could be a useful preliminary to studying the play as a whole to determine

whether the sub-text which is imagined accords with more detailed knowledge of what happened in the past.

Experimenting with pause, whether in scripted or improvised work, can be viewed as a way of using form to contribute to meaning in drama. Bolton (1992: 20) has pointed out that many of the devices the dramatist/ actor uses on stage are those we use in 'real life': '. . . imagine an authority figure who requires us to walk across the room to his desk (he is manipulating space) where he keeps us standing. Then he allows a silence to fall before answering our request (he is manipulating time). In both of these examples the authority figure is using form to enhance the meaning of the situation.' Paradoxically, however, some elements of form used in 'real life' are less, rather than more, likely to be used in 'living through' drama.

The use of pause, whether to create tension or for some other reason, is less likely to feature in spontaneous work than in planned improvisations. It perhaps has its most natural home in scripted work. The reason for this is that a pause or silence in spontaneous drama is more likely to be ambiguous and may be interpreted as signalling an uncertainty about how to advance the drama. The more enthusiastic and committed a group are, the more keen they are likely to be to keep the meaning unfolding. Similarly, decision-making in spontaneous drama may appear to involve the group in confronting a moral dilemma, but in reality may have more to do with advancing the plot (Fleming, 1994: 18). When pupils do use formal elements in the course of spontaneous work it may well be an indication of the high sense of dramatic form that they have which can be developed by examining the use of pause in other contexts.

As indicated above, work on scripted extracts is useful because it allows the group to experiment with different approaches to the same text. The scene immediately after the murder of Duncan in *Macbeth* lends itself to precisely this kind of treatment.

MACBETH: I have done the deed. Didst thou not hear a noise?
LADY MACBETH: I heard the owl scream and the crickets cry. Did you not speak?
MACBETH: When?
LADY MACBETH: Now.
MACBETH: As I descended?
LADY MACBETH: Ay.
MACBETH: Hark, who lies i' th' second chamber?
LADY MACBETH: Donalbain.
MACBETH: This is a sorry sight.
LADY MACBETH: A foolish thought, to say a sorry sight.

An extract from the screenplay of *Langrishe, Go Down* (quoted by Griffiths, 1982) is also appropriate for experimenting with silences and exploring sub-text. Helen has just stolen Imogen's love letters but the latter cannot bring herself to challenge her:

IMOGEN: Oh Helen . . .

(HELEN *stops*)

HELEN: Yes? what is it?

IMOGEN: Could I have a word with you?

HELEN: Surely.

(HELEN *walks up towards her*)

HELEN: What is it?

(*Pause*)

IMOGEN: I was just wondering . . . why you . . . I mean . . . if you . . .

(*Pause*)

HELEN: If I what?

(*Pause*)

IMOGEN: Well, I just wondered . . .

Pupils can also be encouraged to experiment with pause as a way of injecting extra tension into planned improvised work, as long as the dangers of creating too much artificiality are avoided. The following examples indicate different types of contexts which might be appropriate:

- the pupil has to knock twice on the head teacher's door before being asked to enter;
- the parcel which has arrived unexpectedly is inspected with great care before it is slowly opened;
- while the rest of the group wait to hear what the prospects are of getting back to base, the leader carefully folds the map and puts it away;
- before answering the question put by her parent, the daughter gets up and looks out of the window;
- before giving his decision, the king walks slowly to his throne and sits down;
- before going on her journey through the woods, Red Riding Hood slowly packs her basket.

It may be helpful, then, to summarise the different purposes for deliberately using pause and silence in drama, whether the work is with or without script. It helps to slow down the acting, to create or increase the tension or uncertainty, to symbolise inability to communicate, to draw attention to the importance of sub-text.

Explicit attention to pauses and silences within drama is also a useful way of exploring the nature of dramatic language and the contrast between language in drama and language in everyday life. Drama tends to employ language in an unnatural way. As Elam (1980: 91) has pointed out, dialogue exchange in drama tends to be organised in an ordered manner, unlike the 'give-and-take of social intercourse'. This was considered in Chapter 10 in the context of a discussion of the use of overlapping speech. Paradoxically, the language of spontaneous 'living through' drama will often bear less relationship to real life language than some forms of scripted work which can seek to emulate the silences, pauses, false starts and *non sequiturs* which are characteristic of real speech. Using pause is part of the deliberate and conscious construction of drama.

CHAPTER TWENTY

Play Within A Play

Enter the clowns: QUINCE, BOTTOM, SNUG, FLUTE, SNOUT *and* STARVELING

BOTTOM: Are we all met?

QUINCE: Pat, Pat; and here's a marvellous convenient place for our rehearsal. This green plot shall be our stage, this hawthorn brake our tiring-house, and we will do it in action as we will do it before the Duke.

BOTTOM: Peter Quince!

QUINCE: What sayest thou, bully Bottom?

BOTTOM: There are things in this comedy of Pyramus and Thisbe that will never please. First, Pyramus must draw a sword to kill himself, which the ladies cannot abide. How answer you that?

SNOUT: By'r lakin, a parlous fear!

STARVELING: I believe we must leave the killing out, when all is done.

BOTTOM: Not a whit. I have a device to make all well. Write me a prologue, and let the prologue seem to say we will do no harm with our swords, and that Pyramus is not killed indeed; and for the more better assurance, tell them that I, Pyramus, am not Pyramus, but Bottom the weaver. This will put them out of fear.

QUINCE: Well, we will have such a prologue, and it shall be written in eight and six.

BOTTOM: No, make it two more; let it be written in eight and eight.

SNOUT: Will not the ladies be afeard of the lion?

STARVELING: I fear it, I promise you.

BOTTOM: Masters, you ought to consider with yourself: to bring in – God shield us! – a lion among ladies is a most dreadful thing; for there is not a more fearful wild-fowl than your lion living; and we ought to look to 't.

SNOUT: Therefore another prologue must tell he is not a lion.

BOTTOM: Nay, you must name his name, and half his face must be seen through the lion's neck, and he himself must speak through, saying thus, or to the same defect: 'Ladies', or 'Fair ladies – I would wish you' or 'I would request you' or 'I would entreat you – not to fear, not to tremble. My life for yours: if you think I come hither as a lion, it were pity of my life. No, I am no such thing. I am a man as other men are.' – And there indeed let him name his name, and tell them plainly he is Snug the joiner.

QUINCE: Well, it shall be so. But there is two hard things: that is, to bring the moonlight into a chamber – for, you know, Pyramus and Thisbe meet by moonlight.

SNUG: Doth the moon shine that night we play our play?

BOTTOM: A calendar, a calendar! Look in the almanac – find out moonshine, find out moonshine!

QUINCE: Yes, it doth shine that night.

BOTTOM: Why, then may you leave a casement of the Great Chamber window – where we play – open, and the moon may shine in at the casement.

QUINCE: Ay; or else one must come in with a bush of thorns and a lantern, and say he comes to disfigure, or to present, the person of Moonshine . . .

William Shakespeare, A Midsummer Night's Dream

Commentary

The play which the mechanicals are discussing in this extract prior to their rehearsal is performed in the final scene of *A Midsummer Night's Dream* to celebrate the marriage of Theseus and Hippolyta. They have chosen the love story of *Pyramus and Thisbe* which, while providing enormous potential for comedy, parallels the situation of the main action.

In the first scene of Act 3 the mechanicals are in the wood where the 'tiring-house' or 'dressing room' is provided by the hawthorn thicket. Before starting to rehearse they rather ludicrously come to the view that the play they have picked has content (a character who commits suicide with his own sword and a lion) which might frighten the audience. The solution they come up with is equally ridiculous: they will insert a prologue explaining to the audience that all is in fact make-believe. Furthermore, they will make sure that the face of the actor playing the lion is only half covered, and he likewise will let the audience know he is a man. One source of the humour is the disparity between the performance of the mechanicals and the naiveté of the assumptions they make about its potential affect on the audience. The play the mechanicals will rehearse and perform takes place within Shakespeare's play. Through the device of 'play within a play', Shakespeare is able to parody a particular type of romantic comedy, provide a parallel with the main action, interlink with the central plot and comment on the process of drama and the nature of dramatic art. When the mechanicals' play is finally performed the reaction of the on-stage audience is as important as the play itself. Their level of awareness and sophistication goes beyond that of the actors and they amuse themselves with comments during the play. However, the perspective of the on-stage audience is wider still because they are able to discern the comic parody of the central action of the main play. Styan (1975: 29) has commented, that 'when the lovers, an on-stage audience, ridicule the clowns who parody their sentiments in the play-within-the-play, we the off-stage audience, see both groups in satisfying perspective'. And yet the sight of the limited perception of the on-stage audience may serve as a reminder that it is easy enough for any audience to have a blinkered vision. The play within a play convention, because it is itself a comment on the nature of dramatic art, enriches the meaning and ambiguity of the play.

The device at its most simple involves one group of dramatic figures performing a play for another group. Because there is a double framing at work (the audience is observing actors pretending to be dramatic figures who are in turn pretending to be someone else) it can work as a distancing device. The fact that the subject of the drama is another drama means the technique is a form of meta-theatricality whereby the relationship between the audience and theatre is highlighted and even specifically discussed. In *A Midsummer Night's Dream* there is not only consideration of the effect the play will have on the audience (as in this extract), there is also discussion of props and setting, how to depict moonlight and represent a wall. Because the play within a play is framed differently (the audience looks at it through the perspective of the other figures) it allows for different acting styles and language; in the Pyramus and Thisbe example, the mechanicals are differentiated by their prose, but within the play itself they use an exaggerated romantic language and declamatory style of acting which is a source of the humour and satire.

For all its humour, the extract here can be seen as a comment on the aesthetics of the drama process itself. The mechanicals recognise that the aim of the drama is not to convince the audience that what they are watching is real, neither is it to provoke in them real emotions. The absurdity and humour, of course, derive from the ludicrous idea that the mechanicals' play might run the risk of doing just that. Nevertheless, they are essentially recognising that entry into a fictional world is central to the process of drama.

Play within a play is a particular way of framing the action so that it is viewed through the eyes of another set of dramatic figures in the play.

Other forms of framing, then – as for example, when one set of characters eavesdrop on another (*Othello*) or when one group set out to make sure their conversation is being overheard by another group (*Much Ado About Nothing*) – could be described as belonging to the same broad category of play within a play. O'Neill (1995: 127) rightly claims that tableaux can operate in the same way because they can 'reflect or criticise the apparent values of the work'. She goes on to point out that the effect of devices of this kind is 'to implicate the spectators as voyeurs and to heighten their consciousness of their dual function as participants and critical observers.'

Sometimes the convention is used as a 'presentational device' (Elam, 1988: 90), similar to a prologue which serves to introduce the main drama as in the case of *The Taming of the Shrew*. Here in the introduction or prologue, a group of Lords play a trick on the drunken tinker, Sly, and the subsequent comedy is performed for him. However, once the main play has started there is very little comment from the on-stage audience – many productions do not have them present beyond the first scene.

The device of play within a play then can allow
• a different style of acting behaviour
• a different dramatic form
• distancing
• refocusing
• reflection on the drama process itself
• an introduction to the main drama.

Examples

Like the dramatist, the drama teacher and pupils creating drama can employ the convention to allow different styles and forms of language within one play. 'Process' drama which is often employed in drama in education can have within it enacted scenes which are more product-oriented (using different forms of depiction) as in the examples below:
• An RE teacher wanted to enact a scene in which someone has to attempt to talk down a member of the public who is threatening suicide. The scene was much easier to enact when it was placed within a training context. The pupils took the part of police on a course and the scene itself was, within the drama, meant to be a simulation. This made it much easier for the pupils to believe in the scene and paradoxically the distance created a more realistic depiction of such an event.
• A play about a shipwreck worked better when it was reconstructed in the television studio. Previous attempts had been chaotic because the

involvement in the immediacy of the action was not sufficiently controlled. The teacher interviewed the survivors of the shipwreck months after the event in a television studio and they proceeded to recreate the events of the night in question.

- Various forms of documentary drama can be seen as adaptations of the play within a play technique, because they allow the use of different framing devices and therefore different conventions, e.g. the enactment of a scene from the Fire of London is framed within the context of a television documentary (see Chapter 10: Incongruity). A play about a robbery or murder can be framed within a 'rough justice' documentary style which questions whether the right person has been punished for the crime. Thus the pupils can be asked to consider the moral dilemma while still enjoying the challenge of recreating the crime.

- As archaeologists, investigators or historians the participants recreate the way a particular object might have been used in the past (see Chapter 17: Object Focus). Play within a play (in its broadest sense) is employed in Heathcote's mantle of the expert approach. Pupils adopted the role of modern day beekeepers who had been asked to work with bees using early methods (Heathcote and Bolton, 1995: 118).

- As part of a Personal and Social Education lesson on the theme of bullying, the pupils, instead of tackling the subject matter directly in drama, adopt the roles of people who are making video programmes on the topic. The scenes of bullying which are depicted are rehearsed and directed within the overall dramatic structure.

- A group of pupils who are studying *Macbeth* create a play about members of a school or youth club who are putting on a production of the play. The rivalries, ambitions and attempts to usurp position have parallels with Shakespeare's play. *Living With Lady Macbeth* (Rob John), a modern play text based on this idea, is accessible to pupils and uses a range of dramatic conventions.

The following drama used the play within a play convention as part of a project on cultural awareness. The leader had the luxury of a group of postgraduate student teachers to work with the class of 14 year olds but it could be adapted for the normal classroom.

1. The teachers acted a short scene which established that a group of aliens (anthropologists) were visiting earth to research the lives of the inhabitants. The convention of a 'language device' (a small box worn on the belt) allowed the aliens to tune in to the host language so that their initial incomprehensible exchanges (which established their alien identity) gave way to them speaking in English.

2. The scene was humorous and entertaining and established the dramatic frame more quickly than an extended discussion. The initial signing had to be very simple and stylised without trying to be naturalistic. Using costume for the aliens, providing contextual details such as name of planet, life-style, technical expertise would have been inappropriate. It was important that the drama did not try too hard to be convincing (consider the parallels with the mechanicals in Shakespeare's play who think their play might be mistaken for reality). The purpose of the initial performance was to lay down the 'rules of the game' not to create belief.

3. The convention of 'video' allowed the aliens to receive reports from their researchers on earth as a form of play within a play. Everyday earth scenes were shown (e.g. a dentist's waiting room and surgery, a modern office) and the aliens sought to make sense of what they saw. All this was observed by the pupils who simply formed an off-stage audience and were not yet in role. Again, it was important that the scene did not try too hard at realism. The whole scenario of aliens visiting earth and reporting back had to be accepted, as well as the unlikely idea that an intelligent race would be confounded by simple objects and customs. These conventions were established in the initial performance and facilitated by the play within a play approach.

4. A brief teacher-led discussion followed the initial presentation which considered how the misunderstandings which were central to the drama could be a source of entertainment and humour but could also provide a deeper commentary on aspects of human life.

5. The task for the pupils was to create their own scenes (again as plays within a play) which would similarly be read and interpreted by an alien race. The pupils now assumed the roles of both aliens and earthlings. This was crucial to the process of 'defamiliarisation' which was central to the drama – they were being asked to look at familiar events in a new light. The 'play within a play' convention helped to establish the two required levels: the presentation of the 'video recorded' scene and the commentary which was also enacted in role. There were similarly two levels of engagement with the make-believe – the scenes from earth were more crafted and rehearsed, while the scenes in which the aliens analysed the recordings were more exploratory and open-ended.

CHAPTER TWENTY-ONE

Reported Action

CHORUS:	Already we have wept enough for the things we have known,
	The things we have seen. What more will your story add?
ATTENDANT:	First, and in brief – Her Majesty is dead.
CHORUS:	Alas, poor soul: what brought her to this end?
ATTENDANT:	Her own hand did it. You that have not seen,

And shall not see, this worst, shall suffer the less.
But I that saw, will remember, and will tell what I remember
Of her last agony.
    You saw her cross the threshold
In desperate passion. Straight to her bridal-bed
She hurried, fastening her fingers in her hair.
There in her chamber, the doors flung sharply to,
She cried aloud to Laius long since dead,
Remembering the son she bore long since, the son
By whom the sire was slain, the son to whom
The mother bore yet other children, fruit
Of luckless misbegetting. There she bewailed
The twice confounded issue of her wifehood –
Husband begotten of husband, child of child.
So much we heard. Her death was hidden from us.
Before we could see out her tragedy,
The King broke in with piercing cries, and all
Had eyes only for him. This way and that
He strode among us. 'A sword, a sword!' he cried;
'Where is that wife, no wife of mine – that soil
Where I was sown, and whence I reaped my harvest!'
While thus he raved, some demon guided him –
For none of us dared speak – to where she was.
As if in answer to some leader's call

With wild hallooing cries he hurled himself
Upon the locked doors, bending by main force
The bolts out of their sockets – and stumbled in.
   We saw a knotted pendulum, a noose,
A strangled woman swinging before our eyes.
   The King saw too, and with heart-rending groans
Untied the rope, and laid her on the ground.
But worse was yet to see. Her dress was pinned
With golden brooches, which the King snatched out
And thrust, from full arm's length, into his eyes –
Eyes that should see no longer his shame, his guilt,
No longer see those they should never have seen,
Nor see, unseeing, those he had longed to see,
Henceforth seeing nothing but night . . . To this wild tune
He pierced his eyeballs time and time again,
Till bloody tears ran down his beard – not drops
But in full spate a whole cascade descending
In drenching cataracts of scarlet rain.

Sophocles, King Oedipus

Commentary

This scene occurs near the end of Sophocles' tragedy based on the well-known legend of Oedipus. After his birth an oracle foretold that Oedipus would one day kill his father (Laius) and marry his mother (Jocasta). A servant who was ordered to expose the child and leave it to perish did not have the heart to do so and gave it instead to a shepherd. Oedipus was therefore taken and brought up beyond the borders of Thebes. Unaware of his own origins, Oedipus did indeed return to his homeland and fulfil the prophecy. The consequences of the final revelation of the truth are presented in this scene as the queen (his mother and wife) commits suicide and Oedipus puts out his own eyes. In keeping with the convention, the actual events are reported rather than depicted on stage.

   The theory of drama in Aristotle's *Poetics* included the idea that it was not necessary to witness terrible events which aroused horror on stage. 'Spectacle', the showing of the events, is neither necessary nor artistic. It is enough for events to be reported (as in *Oedipus*) for the emotions to be aroused. The account of the deeds may be more effective than their actual enactment. The effect of the technique of reported action is partly aesthetic because actions are presented in a more oblique and distanced way. It is also sometimes described as having a more pragmatic function in that events which are difficult to depict on stage may be reported.

In this extract the strength of the language and the graphic description are extremely powerful. Notice that the actual account of the queen's suicide is in a sense twice removed because not even the servant reporting the events was witness to them, 'So much we heard. Her death was hidden from us.' The image of the servant outside the room listening to her cries when Oedipus arrives is very moving. The drama is intense because the servant is using the first person, reporting what he himself has experienced. The events are distanced but the power of their description makes them hardly less vivid.

The actual structure of Sophocles' play does not follow the full chronology of the legend. The play dramatises the last twenty-four hours of Oedipus' life but the events of the myth are given as the play unfolds through various duologues. Thus the story of how Oedipus killed his father is given in the conversation between Creon and Oedipus at the start of the play. It is much later, by questioning the shepherd, that Oedipus learns what happened to him at birth which of course chronologically comes much earlier in the story. These exchanges are also forms of reported action which provide enormous potential for dramatic irony.

At the start of the play the pestilence and famine which Thebes is suffering, and the previous history of events when Oedipus arrived to free the city from the power of the Sphinx, is described by the priest:

PRIEST: It was you, we remember, a newcomer to Cadmus' town,
That broke our bondage to the vile Enchantress.

Soon after the beginning of the first scene, Creon enters in order to bring news of why the city is now suffering:

CREON: We had a king, sir, before you came to lead us.
His name was Laius.
OEDIPUS: I know. I never saw him.
CREON: He was killed. And clearly the meaning of the god's command
Is that we bring the unknown killer to justice.

The unknown killer is of course Oedipus, and the full history of the previous years is unfolded in the course of the play, largely through reports from different characters.

Thus reported action can be used to provide a non-linear dramatic structure for the creation of plot out of narrative, as well as to describe events which happen in the course of the normal chronology of the drama (as in the longer extract from the play). It can also be used at the beginning of a play as a means of exposition when earlier events which have a bearing on the action are described. The events of J. M. Synge's *Playboy of the Western World* span less than a day and the setting of a public house remains the same in each scene. The action on which the plot revolves, therefore, is reported by the main character with the added twist that what he reports is not exactly the way things happened. He wrongly thinks he has killed his father and the adulation he receives is ironically misplaced.

> CHRISTY: . . . I just riz the loy and let fall the edge of it on the ridge of his skull, and he went down at my feet like an empty sack, and never let a grunt or groan from him at all.

The use of reported action is a feature of many dramatic texts. In *Macbeth*, the death of Lady Macbeth is reported but the other acts of violence (e.g. the killing of Banquo and Macduff's wife and children) are portrayed on stage. The reporting of Lady Macbeth's death allows the focus to be on Macbeth's reaction as in the 'tomorrow and tomorrow and tomorrow' speech. In *King Lear* the blinding of Gloucester is shown on stage, but the hanging of Cordelia is reported; the impact of her death, however, could hardly be greater. The moment when Lear enters carrying the body of Cordelia has been described as 'one of the most famous and heart rending scenes in world drama' (Bain, Morris and Smith, 1996: 194). At this point the audience do not need to be informed of what has happened because Edmund has just explained the order he gave earlier:

> EDMUND: He hath commission from thy wife and me
> To hang Cordelia in the prison and
> To lay the blame upon her own despair,
> That she fordid herself.

This example points to another method of using reported action in that the audience is not so much given new information as shown which of two courses of action has taken place.

Synge's *Riders to the Sea* has no scene divisions and no conventional dramatic structure. The play is set in the kitchen of a cottage in the west of Ireland and there is very little action on-stage. The deaths of the sons which constitute the centre of the drama are all reported. This allows the drama to focus on death and reaction to death rather than on the individual tragedies. The main protagonist therefore is the mother, Maurya, and the central focus her reaction to the deaths of her sons. The play ends with her

final words, 'No man at all can be living for ever, and we must be satisfied.'

To summarise, then, a dramatist may use reported action for a variety of
reasons:

- as a means of beginning a play;
- as a way of structuring the plot and using different time scales;
- in order to distance events;
- as a way of introducing irony;
- as the central means of structuring a play;
- as a way of concentrating on a character's reactions to events.

Examples

Reported action can be described as a form of off-stage action but there are
crucial differences between the two conventions as described in this book.
Off-stage action (see Chapter 18) refers to the device whereby simultaneous events which are imagined to be happening off-stage interact with the
events depicted on stage. Off-stage action therefore occurs in the dramatic
present, whereas reported action uses a narrative mode. Although there
are affinities with narration (described in Chapter 16) there are also differences: with reported action the dramatic figure describing events is part
of the main action and interacts with the characters at the time of reporting; the narrator (who may also be a figure in the drama) is not actually
reporting information to the other characters but is summarising it for the
audience.

Reported action has to be used carefully. It can introduce the worst kind
of artificial climax ('the barn's on fire') and does not necessarily make the
drama easier for the participants. It may allow events which are difficult to
depict to be described, but the on-stage actors still have to find a way of
reacting to events. Nevertheless, it can be a useful way of developing the
drama and of exploring aspects of dramatic structure, as in the examples
below.

A type of reported action (usually taking the form of new information
rather than report of action *per se*) often occurs in drama lessons when a
letter, telephone call or messenger serves to move the drama on. The following example (Readman and Lamont, 1994: 108) on the topic of dinosaurs with seven to nine year olds used new information to introduce the
central focus and moral dilemma of the work: who should claim ownership of historical remains which have been found in a country by outsiders? Only a brief summary of the lesson is given here and readers

interested in adapting the idea should read the full version in the BBC publication.

1. In role as British researchers in Mexico, the pupils uncover dinosaur remains (outlines of dinosaurs on paper which have previously been prepared by the teacher).
2. They use their sketches and other information to identify what they have found.
3. It is time for the fossils to be taken back to England when a letter is received from the Mexican government. The letter thanks them for their excellent work but informs them that the remains cannot be removed from the country and will be housed in a museum on the site where they were found. The class have to decide whether they agree or whether they think they should be allowed to take some remains home.
4. Children prepare a newspaper photograph (still picture) and headline on the day the palaeontologists return to Britain.

The key to the lesson is the way in which the class respond to the new information (the 'reported action'). One of the potential problems is that they may find it difficult to see the moral case on the government's side because they have invested much in the discovery. An alternative way of structuring the work is to ask the class to decide outside the drama what attitude they will adopt to the letter in their roles as the researchers. In this way different views can be adopted which do not necessarily correspond to their actual opinions. This would more clearly distinguish the attitude of the class from the roles they have adopted within the fiction, and provide more exploration of the moral question from within the drama.

One of the tensions associated with planning drama is how to engage pupils in decisions about the content, while avoiding too many of the risks involved in not having a clear idea about how the lesson will develop. One possibility is to provide the pupils with a clear *structure* for their work which leaves *them* room for an element of decision-making about content. The constraints placed on them because they have to operate within the parameters set by the form tend to be liberating rather than the reverse. This can be a useful approach to playwrighting when the setting, context, characters, and use of reported action are pre-determined, but when pupils still have considerable control over content. The following are examples of this kind of work.

- A family is at breakfast when a letter arrives. The person who receives the letter tries at first to conceal its contents from the others. When the contents are finally revealed the consequences for the whole family are considerable.

MRS JONES: That sounds like the postman – could you see what it is?
(*John leaves and returns moments later*).
JOHN: It's for Julie (*handing over a letter*).
JULIE: Oh, thanks. I'll open it later.

• A group of young people have planned for a bet to stay in a 'haunted house' overnight. One of the party has left the room where they are planning to sleep in order to go to the toilet. The scene begins with the return of the character who is very obviously shaken and ends with the group deciding to leave the house.

BEN: She's been ages.
ANGELA: She's got more courage than me staying out that long.

(*The door opens and Jackie comes in obviously upset and frightened*).

MIKE: What's the matter with you?

• The arrival of a stranger in a small village pub shatters the tranquillity of the village because of the news which he gradually reveals in the course of the scene.

GEORGE: Not many strangers find their way to this pub when they first come here, it's so out of the way.
STRANGER: It's not my first time here.
GEORGE: I don't think I've met you before, have I?
STRANGER: We never actually met but I remember you very well.

CHAPTER TWENTY-TWO

Ritual

CUCHULAIN: (*speaking while the Women who carry a bowl of fire sing.*)

> I'll take and keep this oath, and from this day
> I shall be what you please, my chicks, my nestlings.
> Yet I had thought you were of those that praised
> Whatever life could make the pulse run quickly,
> Even though it were brief, and that you held
> That a free gift was better than a forced.—
> But that's all over.—I will keep it, too;
> I never gave a gift and took it again.
> If the wild horse should break the chariot-pole,
> It would be punished. Should that be in the oath?

(*Two of the Women, still singing, crouch in front of him holding the bowl over their heads. He spreads his hands over the flame.*)

> I swear to be obedient in all things
> To Conchubar, and to uphold his children.

CONCHUBAR: We are one being, as these flames are one:
> I give my wisdom, and I take your strength.
> Now thrust the swords into the flame, and pray
> That they may serve the threshold and the hearthstone
> With faithful service.

(*The Kings kneel in a semicircle before the two Women and* CUCHULAIN, *who thrusts his sword into the flame. They all put the points of their swords into the flame. The third Woman is at the back near the big door.*)

CUCHULAIN: O pure, glittering ones
> That should be more than wife or friend or mistress,

Give us the enduring will, the unquenchable hope,
The friendliness of the sword!—

(The song grows louder, and the last words ring out clearly. There is a loud knocking at the door, and a cry of 'Open! Open!')

CONCHUBAR: Some king that has been loitering on the way.
Open the door, for I would have all know
That the oath's finished and Cuchulain bound,
And that the swords are drinking up the flame.

(The door is opened by the third Woman, and a Young Man with a drawn sword enters.)

YOUNG MAN: I am of Aoife's country.

(The Kings rush towards him. CUCHULAIN *throws himself between.)*

CUCHULAIN: Put up your swords.
He is but one. Aoife is far away.
YOUNG MAN: I have come alone into the midst of you
To weigh this sword against Cuchulain's sword.
CONCHUBAR: And you are noble? for if of common seed,
You cannot weigh your sword against his sword
But in mixed battle.
YOUNG MAN: I am under bonds
To tell my name to no man; but it's noble.

W. B. Yeats, *On Baile's Strand*

Commentary

In this extract Cuchulain, the central character in the play, takes an oath which is conducted with great ritual and ceremony. To gain insight into the function of the ritualistic element of the drama, the broad context and meaning of the play needs some explanation.

The play is based on the legendary figures of Ireland and the context is set in the first scene during an expository dialogue between a fool and a blind man, figures who parallel the main protagonists, Cuchulain and Conchubar. In the course of the encounter between the minor characters, they let the audience know that King Conchubar is coming that day to persuade Cuchulain to take an oath to 'stop his rambling and make him as biddable as a house-dog'. They also make it known that a young man has arrived to challenge Cuchulain in battle. The stranger is the son of Aoife, a great woman warrior in Scotland whom Cuchulain had previously conquered. Later in the play we learn that he fell in love with her and then left without realising that she was pregnant. The young man, therefore, who on her orders has come to challenge Cuchulain, turns out to be his own son. Neither father nor son have met before because the child was brought up by his mother without Cuchulain's knowledge of his existence. The son who makes his first appearance in this extract is killed by Cuchulain who, on discovering his real identity, rushes out in a mad frenzy to fight the waves of the sea.

In this scene (as foretold by the fool and the blind man) Cuchulain, who has been causing trouble in the kingdom, is in the process of taking an oath to obey Conchubar and bow to his will. At first he is reluctant to comply and is not willing to have his free spirit constrained:

> I'll not be bound.
> I'll dance or hunt, or quarrel or make love,
> Wherever and whenever I've a mind to.

There is a deliberate contrast between the free spirit of Cuchulain and the steadfastness and sobriety of Conchubar who would like to leave a 'strong and settled country' to his children. The play centres on this contrast of opposites. Conchubar is a 'solid bourgeois citizen, timid, prudent, with a shrewd perception of the main chance . . . Cuchulain is the hero of the action' (Donoghue, 1971: 102). The king embodies reason, pragmatism, objectivity, while the hero can be said to symbolise passion and subjectivity. They are paralleled at a more banal level by the fool and blind man who both need each other. As the fool says, 'I would never be able to steal anything if you didn't tell me where to look for it.' After the oath has been sworn, the unity is expressed by Conchubar:

> We are one being, as these flames are one;
> I give my wisdom, and I take your strength.

One of the reasons given for Cuchulain's irresponsibility is that he has no children. He is finally persuaded to take the oath by warriors who were once like him: 'It's you that have changed. You've wives and children now . . .' Two themes of the play, fatherhood and the contrast between freedom and conformity, are central to this extract, and the oath is a key pivot in the structure because it marks Cuchulain's acquiescence. The scene before the fight is heavy with irony because his instinct is to befriend the young man who reminds him of one 'I had a fancy for'. The oath which binds him to Conchubar means that he has little alternative but to fight.

The ritual which accompanies the oath fulfils a number of functions:

- It helps to evoke a remote, past world which is central to the setting of the play.
- It marks a major turning point in the play because it symbolises the stability which has been achieved in the kingdom. Ironically, Cuchulain fights and kills the stranger (his own son) out of deference to Conchubar's will.
- It slows down the action of the drama making it more deliberate and emphasising this as a turning point in the play.
- It provides a contrast with the terrible events which will follow. The change is marked by the sudden knocking on the door.
- It emphasises the more abstract, poetic and symbolic quality of the drama in which ideas are more important than character development.

Ritual is used within *On Baile's Strand* but the play as a whole can be seen as highly ritualistic, particularly in its use of language. In 1899 Yeats declared that the 'theatre began in ritual, and it cannot come to its greatness again without recalling words to their ancient sovereignty'. (Rajan, 1965: 59). There are similarities with Brook's comment in *The Empty Space* (1968: 50) when he expressed his dissatisfaction with many contemporary forms of theatre: 'Even if the theatre had in its origins rituals that made the visible incarnate, we must not forget that apart from certain Oriental theatres these rituals have either been lost or remain in seedy decay.' Artaud and Grotowski similarly turned to ritual to revive the theatre.

According to Schechner (1993: 228), ritual manifests itself in many aspects of human and animal behaviour. His definition in *The Future of Ritual* is derived from ethology: 'ritual is ordinary behaviour transformed by means of condensation, exaggeration, repetition, and rhythm into specialised sequences of behaviour serving specific functions usually having to do with mating, hierarchy or territoriality'. He goes on to describe the evolutionary development of ritual from those examples which are genetically fixed, as in the case of insects and fish, to the higher social, religious and aesthetic human rituals. Edwards (1976: 10) begins his account of ritual and the theatre with an examination of the ritualistic elements in the behaviour of football supporters, drawing attention to the conformity to particular patterns, the rhythmical chanting. 'We call this behaviour a ritual because it takes place on a special occasion and because it conforms to a pattern which is regulated and accepted by common consent of all who take part in it'. Drama, because it has its origins in religious ceremony, is seen by some writers as a manifestation of a human propensity for ritual.

As these examples indicate, the concept of ritual is used variously and is potentially confusing. It may be helpful to distinguish between:

1. The identification of all drama as a manifestation of a natural human inclination towards ritual;
2. The use of the term 'ritual' to describe a particular form or style of drama;
3. The use of ritual within drama.

Esslin (1978: 10) recognised that drama can be seen as 'a manifestation of the play instinct' or 'as a manifestation of one of humanity's prime social needs, that of ritual.' In the context of drama teaching, seeing ritual as a natural human inclination is a helpful corrective to the tendency to see the origins of children's drama as being purely in spontaneous dramatic play. Writing in 1966, Bolton recognised the difference between the open-ended spontaneous activity of make-believe play and the inclination to ritualise which also characterises young children's involvement with dramatic activity, when for example they repeatedly act out a story. "What in fact appears to be rapid deterioration to the teacher has become a ritual packed with inner meaning akin, not to make believe play, but to children's street games like ring-a-ring of roses or 'What time is it, Mr Wolf?'" Children's inclination to condense, repeat and exaggerate can be exploited when devising drama just as much as their propensity for dramatic play.

Hornbrook (1991) has criticised the reductive tendencies of some of the school drama of the 1970s and 1980s which concentrated purely on attempts at naturalistic improvisation of social issues. Recognition of ritual as a way of describing a particular approach to drama or as a convention within drama is a reminder of the alternative approaches available. Ritual has always been an ingredient in the practice of the most distinguished advocates of drama in education.

Examples

Morgan and Saxton (1987: 132) helpfully identify opportunities for using ritual within drama in the context for example of: departures (e.g. leaving on a journey, death, arming oneself), arrival (e.g. arriving in a new land, marking territory), celebrations (e.g. a toast, acknowledging achievements), dedications/affirmations (e.g. swearing an oath, signing a contract), procedure (e.g. calling the roll, reading a will).

The following lessons drawn from various practitioners illustrate the way in which ritualistic elements can be used in drama:

• The drama was based on the poem *Flannan Isle* (W. W. Gibson) which tells the story of three lighthouse keepers who mysteriously disappeared without trace. The project culminated in an investigation into what might have happened to the men. In the first activity, the pupils are asked to imagine that they are men from the *Hesperus,* the boat sent to find out why the light was not shining. When they land they are each asked to imagine that they bring back one object from the lighthouse which might give a clue to what has happened. These are ritualistically placed in the centre of a circle and each pupil is invited to justify why he/she has chosen to bring the particular object. (Rankin, 1995: 44)

- In a drama about a group of space travellers marooned on a planet for many years, they gather to remind each other of some custom from Earth which they must remember if they are to remain a civilised community (Neelands, 1990: 40). This example is interesting because it involves both a use of ritual in the drama and a conscious awareness of the role of ritual in society. It prompts the question, 'What is it about these activities which, although they may have no obvious functional value, makes them worth preserving ?'
- In the following example, in order to introduce the topic for the drama which was set in the past, the teacher used ritual to establish both the roles and atmosphere (O'Neill et al, 1976). The king (teacher in role) sat the class in a circle (an appropriate shape for ritual), asked them to take their swords from their belts in order to salute and invited each in turn to tell a story about their strength and courage. After a display of strength, the king then chose the chief knight in ritualistic fashion by walking slowly twice around the circle to heighten the tension.
- A drama based on work on the Saxons included a formal meeting of the villagers in which no one could speak unless holding the 'sacred sword of Thor' (Kitson and Spiby, 1995: 34). The element of ritual here, similar to the use of the conch in *Lord of the Flies,* has the added advantage of controlling the discussion.
- In a drama with six/seven year olds based on the Nativity, Bolton (1992: 83) used ritual to bring the work to a conclusion. The children had been placed in role as the people who took in Mary and Joseph before the birth (they had to prove in the drama that they knew enough about caring for a baby). The baby was represented by a scarf and the lesson ended with a ritualistic naming and passing of the baby to each person around the circle.
- In a lesson with 14 year olds, the specific objectives were to explore the function of myth, legend and ritual in a tribal community. Students

were asked to build up a picture of the village in discussion, and then to create, first, a myth to explain how the sun, stars and moon originated; then a legend which had been told for hundreds of years in the culture; and, finally, a ritual appropriate to the tribe (Burgess and Gaudry, 1985: 222).

• Ritual can also be used to explore text. The 'Shakespeare in Schools' edition of *King Lear* (Bain et al. 1996: 200) recommends a simple but extremely effective way of making vivid the language of the play at the moment of Cordelia's death. All the phrases and sentences in Act 5, scene 3, lines which express grief or sympathy for Cordelia or Lear, are written on pieces of paper and distributed to the group. These are then memorised and spoken as the mourners assemble around a tableau of Lear and Cordelia. The scene can be made more effective by the use of music and dimmed lights (e.g. candles). A similar technique can be used to explore the final scene of *Romeo and Juliet.*

Ritual is valuable as a technique available to pupils and teachers within the drama lesson, but it also provides an insight into the nature of the art form itself.

CHAPTER TWENTY-THREE

Time Shift

WILLY: I been wondering why you polish the car so careful. Ha! Don't leave the hubcaps, boys. Get the chamois to the hubcaps. Happy, use newspaper on the windows, it's the easiest thing. Show him how to do it, Biff! You see, Happy? Pad it up, use it like a pad! That's it, that's it, good work. You're doin' all right, Hap. (*He pauses, then nods in approbation for a few seconds, then looks upward.*) Biff, first thing we gotta do when we get time is clip that big branch over the house. Afraid it's gonna fall in a storm and hit the roof. Tell you what. We get a rope and sling her around, and then we climb up there with a couple of saws and take her down. Soon as you finish the car, boys, I wanna see ya. I got a surprise for you, boys.

BIFF (*offstage*): Whatta ya got, Dad?

WILLY: No, you finish first. Never leave a job till you're finished – remember that.

(*Looking toward the 'big trees'.*) Biff, up in Albany I saw a beautiful hammock. I think I'll buy it next trip, and we'll hang it right between those two elms. Wouldn't that be something? Just swingin' there under those branches. Boy that would . . .

YOUNG BIFF *and* YOUNG HAPPY *appear from the direction Willy was addressing.* HAPPY *carries rags and a pail of water.* BIFF, *wearing a sweater with a block 'S', carries a football.*

BIFF (*pointing in the direction of the car offstage*): How's that Pop, professional?

WILLY: Terrific. Terrific job, boys. Good work, Biff.

HAPPY: Where's the surprise, Pop?

WILLY: In the back seat of the car.

HAPPY: Boy! (*He runs off.*)

BIFF: What is it, Dad? Tell me, what'd you buy?

WILLY (*laughing, cuffs him*): Never mind, something I want you to have.

BIFF (*turn and starts off*): What is it, Hap?

HAPPY (*offstage*): It's a punching bag!

BIFF: Oh, Pop!

WILLY: It's got Gene Tunney's signature on it!

HAPPY *runs onstage with a punching bag.*

BIFF: Gee, how'd you know we wanted a punching bag?

WILLY: Well, it's the finest thing for the timing.

HAPPY (*lies down on his back and pedals with his feet*): I'm losing weight, you notice, Pop?

WILLY: (*to Happy*): Jumping rope is good too.

BIFF: Did you see the new football I got?

WILLY (*examining the ball*): Where'd you get a new ball?

BIFF: The coach told me to practise my passing.

WILLY: That's so? And he gave you the ball, heh?

BIFF: Well, I borrowed it from the locker room. (*He laughs confidentially.*)

WILLY (*laughing with him at the theft*): I want you to return that.

HAPPY: I told you he wouldn't like it!

BIFF (*angrily*): Well, I'm bringing it back!

WILLY (*stopping the incipient argument, to Happy*): Sure, he's gotta practise with a regulation ball, doesn't he? (*To Biff.*) Coach'll probably congratulate you on your initiative!

BIFF: Oh, he keeps congratulating my initiative all the time, Pop.

WILLY: That's because he likes you. If somebody else took that ball there'd be an uproar. So what's the report, boys, what's the report?

BIFF: Where'd you go this time, Dad? Gee, we were lonesome for you.

WILLY (*pleased, puts an arm around each boy and they come down to the apron*): Lonesome, heh?

BIFF: Missed you every minute.

WILLY: Don't say? Tell you a secret, boys. Don't breathe it to a soul. Someday I'll have my own business, and I'll never have to leave home any more.

Arthur Miller, Death of a Salesman

Commentary

If this extract, from Act One, is read without knowing the context, it seems to depict a fairly ordinary family scene which shows a proud father interacting with his sons. His preoccupation with domestic tasks such as cleaning the car and pruning the tree reinforces the image of him as a family man as does his final comment that soon he will not have to leave home any more. Biff and Happy are eager to please him ('How's that Pop, professional?', 'I'm losing weight, you notice, Pop?'). They seem to enjoy a close relationship with him ('Gee, we were lonesome for you') and he is proud of their achievements. He is a man with legitimate ambitions, 'Someday I'll have my own business'. His surprise present of a punching bag, and his concern to bring his sons up correctly ('Never leave a job till you're finished') could all be seen as different manifestations of the positive and caring relationship he has with them.

A closer reading of the extract might prompt a slightly different interpretation; the father's pride seems to border on excess, his surprise present could be seen as indulgence. He appears all too ready to excuse what is in fact the theft of a football and to acknowledge the boy's popularity with the teacher, ('If somebody else took that ball there'd be an uproar'). Read out of context, the extract has some ambiguity. Within the context of the play, there is much less uncertainty about the author's intention.

What the audience witness here is actually happening inside Willy's head as he recreates the past. The 'real-time' events in the play are based on what is happening to Willy at the age of 62 during an evening and the following day. Prior to this scene which occurs near the start of the play we have seen Willy return from his sales trip, exhausted, disillusioned ('Some people accomplish something') and struggling to cope. Happy and Biff, now in their thirties, are upstairs listening to Willy's return and when the scene focuses on them we learn more details about the strain between father and sons. 'Why does Dad mock me all the time?' asks Biff. The play's meaning derives from interweaving the present with scenes from the past and from Willy's own fantasies. It will eventually end with Willy's suicide, disillusioned by his unfulfilled dreams.

The way Miller uses the convention of time shift in this play is particularly appropriate to his theme, 'The past, as in hallucination, comes back to Willy Loman, not chronologically as in a flashback, but dynamically, with the inner logic of his erupting volcanic unconscious' (Schneider 1949: 18). Juxtaposing the present against memories of the past (and there is some ambiguity about whether all the memories are accurate) dramatises Willy's present disillusionment which is based very effectively on unfulfilled dreams. Welland (1979: 47) has also argued that to speak of the action containing 'flashbacks' is to 'miss the point'. The recalled scenes are not chronological nor are they totally random; they are prompted by associations with the present. The film version of the play is less effective in representing this scene because the present is actually replaced by the past; on stage, the effect is less naturalistic but past and present can be made to blend more easily.

One of the reasons why drama as an art form is so powerful is that it always takes place in the present – real events are acted out before the audience 'here and now'. The dramatist however is clearly not restricted to presenting a time scale which is restricted by the actual performance time. Miller's play shows the last twenty-four hours of Willy's life – events which on stage take the three hours or so needed for the performance. Events are telescoped into those depicted on stage by the use of omissions and elisions. This is such a common convention in the theatre that it is almost entirely taken for granted. By the use of time shift, Miller goes further and presents a much more complicated chronology which also shows earlier events in Willy's life. From the events depicted on stage it would be possible to determine a narrative from the dramatic plot which is presented.

Time shift is taken here to refer to any departure from the linear chronology of the narrative. The plot of *Betrayal* works by presenting the events in reverse order (see Chapter 19). A similar technique is used in *Top Girls* (see Chapter 10). In *Our Town* one of the characters is able to return to a former period of her life (see Chapter 1). In each case, because there is a departure from the normal unfolding of events through cause and effect, a different type of tension is generated which provides an alternative perspective on the action. For example, with a structure which reverses time the audience knows where the action will eventually lead and will therefore see the earlier events in a different light. Time shift invariably involves a change in frame. As a technique for teachers and pupils to use in creating drama, it has the potential to take them away from a preoccupation with narrative development towards the exploration of situations in greater depth.

Examples

The central idea in this extract can be used directly in the creation of improvised or scripted drama which could either be a lead-in to this extract or constitute a piece of work in its own right. Pupils are asked to create a tableau which is called 'the ideal family'. They are then asked to set this against a short monologue by one of the characters set in the 'present' (i.e. years after the events depicted in the tableau) which gives some account of how the promise of the early scene was not realised. The third task is for the pupils to go back to the first tableau and recreate it as a short piece of enacted drama which now provides a subtle indication that things were not quite as they seemed. This is quite a challenging exercise which is best explained by the use of a concrete example such as the following.

- The tableau shows a conventional family with father reading the daughter's school report and with mother and aunt listening with pride. The daughter is sitting looking rather satisfied.
- Mother's monologue reveals that her daughter has dropped out of university and is now living what is in her view a rather unsavoury life far away from home without keeping regularly in contact.
- When the tableau is brought to life, the scene hints at the parents' excessive pressure on their daughter to succeed academically. The audience is left to infer that fear of failure eventually led her to drop out of university.

Because time shift is a useful convention in translating narrative into plot, it can be used to explore fiction in dramatic contexts. Byron (1986: 61) describes an approach to Golding's *Lord of the Flies* in which the drama began at the point where the novel ends when the boys have been rescued by the naval ship. The point, however, was not to continue the story, but to explore the events retrospectively with pupils taking the roles of the rescued boys. A drama based on Hardy's *Tess of the D'Urbervilles* started with a reading of the scene near the end of the novel in which the landlady notices blood dripping from the room above. The police arrive to investigate.

In *Starting Drama Teaching* I suggested that the bald directive to pupils to 'act out a story' which has rightly been discredited in the past, may, as a task, have more to recommend it than is often assumed if pupils have sufficient skill to tackle it successfully. For narrative to be translated into dramatic plot, pupils will need to have a sense of dramatic form which will demand their being able to find a focus and might include experimenting with non-linear time. For example, the parable of the prodigal son could begin with the son returning home, or indeed with the prodigal son telling his version of events to his own children; the story of the Pied Piper might start with the unveiling of the memorial built to commemorate the events. Pupils will need to decide whether to use such techniques as reported action, narrative, or flashback in order to create plot. This process of selection and shaping cannot really happen successfully without testing and increasing pupils' understanding of the original story.

Another form of time shift in drama is to explore events which would in fact take place simultaneously. Ayckbourn's comic trilogy *The Norman Conquests* is based on this idea in which the three plays cover the same weekend family gathering seen from different perspectives. The first scene of the first play is set at 6 p.m. on the Saturday evening in the dining room, the second play begins at 6.30 in the sitting room and the final play is set at 5.30 in the garden. The convention is not dissimilar to off-stage action (see Chapter 18) but instead of the action off-stage being left to the imagination of the audience, it is shown separately. Thus the audience hear a large crash in one scene, but actually witness the events which caused the crash in another play.

The technique of simultaneous action tends to be used in a simpler form when pupils have created small-group work within a broad structure. For example, they may have created a village and are asked to act a typical breakfast scene in each household prior to the main events of the drama: the arrival of a stranger, news of a chemical leak, a proposal to site a by-pass near a village. The performances can be given a little more subtlety by connecting the scenes so that telephone calls or character exits in one scene can be linked with the complementary events in a different household. This could be a way of conveying hypocrisy; what a character says in one scene is very different from the way his/her opinions have come across in another.

A life story (e.g. of a homeless person) is a useful focus for drama because it provides a ready-made linear structure and has clear thematic content, an exploration of how events from the past brought about the present state of affairs. However, it is because the structure presents itself so obviously that pupils can be encouraged to experiment with alternative approaches. The most obvious is a simple flashback technique whereby the first scene takes place near the end of the individual's life. However, more complex experiments with time may seek to conjure up moments from the person's past through associations with the present. Thus the anchor scene may simply be the individual going into a cafe to have a cup of tea – the 'satellite' scenes from the past (a family meal time, wedding reception, etc.) may be triggered by objects and people in the present.

To summarise, then, time shift is helpful in classroom drama because
- It can slow down the action in order to explore motivation, attitudes, feelings.
- It can provide a different element of tension and demonstrate how drama does not have to work purely on the basis of a linear plot.
- It can provide focus because the pupils know where the drama is leading.
- It allows topics to be explored from different angles because time can be telescoped.
- It provides potential for irony and rich levels of meaning.

CHAPTER TWENTY-FOUR

Unspoken Thoughts

A room in Doogan's house. GAR O'DONNELL, *the main character in the play, is denoted by two characters,* PUBLIC (GAR) *and* PRIVATE (GAR). *These represent two views of the one man.* PUBLIC (GAR) *is the man that people see and talk to –* PRIVATE (GAR) *is the unseen man, the man within, the conscience, the secret thoughts.*

PUBLIC: God, my legs are trembling! Kathy . . .

KATE: Anybody at home? Mammy! Daddy!

(PUBLIC *hesitates before entering* DOOGAN's *house.* PRIVATE *is at his elbow, prompting him desperately.*)

PRIVATE: Mr Doogan – Senator Doogan – I want to ask your permission . . . O my God! . . .

KATE: Yo-ho!

PRIVATE: Mrs Doogan, Kate and I have to get married rightaway – Cripes, no! –

KATE: Where is everybody! Yo-ho-yo-ho!

PRIVATE: If the boys could see you now!

(KATE *comes back to him, gives him a quick kiss on the cheek.*)

KATE: Don't look so miserable. Here . . . .(*Fixes his tie*).

PUBLIC: Kathy, maybe we should wait until – until – until next Sunday –

KATE: (*Earnestly*) Remember, it's up to you, entirely up to you.

DOOGAN: (*Off*) That you, Kate?

KATE: (*Rapidly*) You have £20 a week and £5,000 in the bank and your father's about to retire. (*Turning and smiling at* DOOGAN *who has now entered.*) Just Gar and I, Daddy.

(DOOGAN, *Lawyer, Senator, middle forties.*)

DOOGAN: Hello, Gareth. You're a stranger.

PRIVATE: Speak, you dummy you!

KATE: (*Filling in*) Where's Mammy?

DOOGAN: She's watching TV. (*To* GAR.) And how are things with you, Gareth?

PUBLIC: Mr Doogan, I want –

PRIVATE: Go, on.

PUBLIC: I won't be staying long.

DOOGAN: (*to* KATE) Francis arrived when you were out. Took a few days off and decided to come north.

PRIVATE: Cripes!

KATE: He – he's – he's here – now?

DOOGAN: Inside with your mother. Ask them to join us, will you?

(KATE *gives* PUBLIC *a last significant look.*)

KATE: You talk to Daddy, Gar.

PRIVATE: God, I will, I will.

(KATE *goes off right.*)

DOOGAN: You've met Francis King, haven't you, Gareth?

PUBLIC: Yes – yes –

PRIVATE: King of the bloody fairies!

DOOGAN: We don't want to raise Kate's hopes unduly, but strictly between ourselves there's a good chance that he'll get the new dispensary job here.

PUBLIC: Kate's hopes?

DOOGAN: Didn't she tell you? No, I can see she didn't. Of course there's nothing official yet; not even what you might call an understanding. But if this post does fall into his lap, well, her mother and I . . . let's say we're living in hope. A fine boy, Francis; and we've known the Kings, oh, since away back. As a matter of fact his father and I were class-fellows at school . . .

(DOOGAN *goes on and on. We catch an occasional word.*
Meantime PRIVATE *has moved up to* PUBLIC's *elbow.*)

PRIVATE: Cripes, man!

DOOGAN: . . . and then later at university when he did medicine and I did law, we knocked about quite a bit . . .

PRIVATE: O God, the aul bitch! Cripes, you look a right fool standing there – the father of fourteen children! Get out, you eejit you! Get out! Get out quick before the others come in and die laughing at you! And all the time she must have known – the aul bitch! And you promised to give her breakfast in bed every morning! And you told her about the egg money!

Brian Friel, *Philadelphia, Here I Come*

Commentary

In *Philadelphia, Here I Come* the author has written two parts for the central character, one to articulate his public comments and the other to give voice to his private thoughts. Because both characters are on stage for the entire play we are given what amounts to an insight into his 'inner life'. The content of the play is at one level straightforward – the central character Gareth O'Donnell (Gar) is anticipating his new life when he emigrates to America, but one of the central themes of the play is the tension he feels as a result of his decision to leave, expressed though the two voices of private and public Gar. He is torn between, on the one hand, the desire to escape, to expand his horizons, to assert his independence, and on the other hand, his affection for his country and the emotional loyalties to his family and background.

This extract from Episode One is actually presented as a flashback. Gar is recalling his attempt at informing Kate's parents of his plans to marry her. He nervously rehearses what he will say to them with his private self prompting the public figure to take courage. When Kate leaves the room the father manipulatively points out that there is already someone whom his daughter is likely to marry. When the scene returns to the present, we learn that Gar's plans to marry were not fulfilled as his private self muses wearily, 'Mrs Doctor Francis King. September 8th. In harvest sunshine. Red carpet and white lilies . . .'

The events depicted in the flashback are actually conjured up by private Gar because public Gar wants to suppress the memory which is humiliating to him. Public pretends not to hear him, as private reminds him of the past, 'Remember that was Kate's tune. You needn't pretend you have forgotten. And it reminds you of the night the two of you made all the plans.' Public Gar still carries a photograph of Kate in his wallet and thinks of her fondly, 'my darling Kathy Doogan'. It is private Gar who expresses the conflicting feelings about her ('Aul bitch') and is brutally honest about the memory of that night, 'By God, you made a right bloody cow's ass of yourself.'

The extract and the other quotations from the play indicate that Friel is using the convention of giving voice to unspoken thoughts in a more subtle way than the phrase might suggest. It is not simply a case of one character presenting the words spoken aloud and the other articulating the actual thoughts, as if the private self is what the character really thinks. What we have in the utterances of the two characters is an expression of tension, an inner turmoil. They are able to engage in dialogue with each other and express contradictory and confusing thoughts. The final lines of the play capture the inner conflict and uncertainty very poignantly,

> PRIVATE: God, boy, why do you have to leave?
> PUBLIC: I don't know. I – I – I don't know.

One of the constraints within which drama works which distinguishes it from narrative fiction is the difficulty of conveying what is going on within a character's mind. The thoughts and emotions of characters are normally presented not through commentary, as in narrative fiction, but through the words and actions of the characters. It is, however, the medium of direct speech which gives to drama 'a great part of its cogency and power' (Ellis-Fermor, 1945: 97). This very limitation is a source of its strength as an art form.

There are, therefore, dangers in trying to circumvent the limitations of the form which arise when thought processes are over-simplified. Because normally in drama we do not have access to characters' inner thoughts, these have to be inferred from actions which can make for a more subtle representation of what the character might actually be feeling or thinking at any one time. In reality, the inner life of human beings is not clear-cut, and an element of ambiguity can be preserved by not attempting to reveal their thoughts directly. If one of the strengths of drama lies in its directness, in its use of direct speech, paradoxically, this is also a function of the way it works obliquely, because the corresponding thoughts are concealed. Friel's play is engaging because it does not oversimplify the main character's thought processes.

The use of asides and soliloquies (made easier by the physical design of the Elizabethan stage) are among the more familiar techniques used by dramatists to give voice to inner thoughts. It is significant that the great soliloquies in drama are often quite complex expressions of inner turmoil. Hamlet's 'To be or not to be . . .' speech is an obvious example. Macbeth, before killing Duncan, articulates his uncertainty in the speech, 'If 'twere done when 'tis done'. Before taking the potion which will put her to sleep, Juliet expresses her dilemma and fears through the power of the poetry. In each case the convention is not naturalistic – even if someone were to speak their inner thoughts aloud the conflict would hardly be expressed with such clarity. The soliloquy is one of the times when what a character speaks is to be taken at face value: 'The characters do not deceive themselves or their audience in uttering them; soliloquies express the true feelings and thoughts of those speaking' (Banks, 1991: 148).

Examples

With older pupils the extract itself is useful for introducing the idea of expressing 'unspoken thoughts'. As a way into the play as a whole, pupils can be given this extract with the indicators 'private' and 'public' deleted and can be asked to try to work out which of Gar's utterances come under each category. The exercise reveals that the two aspects of Gar are not so easily distinguished throughout the text and reinforces the view that the distinction is not a crude 'Jekyll and Hyde' division.

Having gained some insight into the technique as used by Friel, pupils can experiment with their own script-writing using the same idea. Possible scenarios include: a worker asking his boss for a rise, someone being interviewed for a job by a panel, a young soldier saying good-bye to his family. In each case the public and private manifestations of the first character are dramatised with serious or humorous possibilities. In the following example, a new teacher is interviewing a pupil for misbehaving in class:

PUBLIC: Right, what was all that about?
PRIVATE: God what a pathetic start – be a bit more assertive.
PUBLIC: Stand up straight when I'm talking to you.
PRIVATE: That's even worse – you're not in the army.
PUPIL: I didn't do anything – I'm going.
PRIVATE: Don't let him leave, you wimp.

The technique of having characters articulate their thoughts, or 'thought-tracking', is common in the drama literature – perhaps almost rivalling tableau as one of the most frequently used conventions. In fact its use is often recommended as an accompaniment to tableau. Characteristically, pupils are given the task of creating a still image (e.g. of an act of bullying) and the teacher will ask each participant by tapping them on the shoulder to articulate his or her thoughts at that particular moment in the drama. It is not my intention to criticise this practice but simply to sound a warning note about its use and to suggest additional ways of using the convention.

One of the disadvantages of the technique is that it may suggest that human motivation is always simple and clear-cut. If we take the bullying example, it may be an unhelpful simplification to impute one single motive to the bully which the exercise can easily prompt pupils into giving. An alternative approach would be to invite a number of pupils (perhaps those watching) to speak the possible thoughts of one of the bullies. These may be contradictory or conflicting but that very fact gives more richness to the situation and leads to discussion of whether motives are ever all that clear-cut.

In the same way, the activity of supplying sub-text to script or improvised drama (in the form of inner thoughts, described in Chapters 9 and 19) may result in a reductive account of a character's feelings and motivations. When the words of a dramatic figure are clearly intended to deceive and are deliberately at odds with what is being thought at a particular moment in the drama, then there is little danger of this happening. When a character like Iago says, 'I do love Cassio well', we know he means the opposite. However, when ambiguity and uncertainty underpin a character's words and behaviour, the supplying of sub-text in the form of inner thoughts may oversimplify the meaning. To avoid this, one alternative is to invite different groups to create sub-texts, to share different interpretations and consider which might be most appropriate. Another approach is to adapt the convention used by Friel of two voices in conflict with each other underpinning the main spoken text.

Take as an example the following dialogue between a parent and teenager. The latter has been caught shoplifting. She has been brought home by the police and let off with a warning. A possible simple sub-text in the form of private thoughts is given in italics.

MOTHER: I knew something like this would happen.
(*God, what are the neighbours going to say about this? I can't stand the shame of it.*)
DAUGHTER: What do you mean?
(*She always thinks she knows everything about me.*)
MOTHER: You're going to have to tell your father when he comes home.
(*I don't know how to deal with this – I'll have to leave it to him.*)
DAUGHTER: What do you mean, 'you knew'?
(*I bet she thinks Julie was with me.*)
MOTHER: You never tell us where you're going or what you're doing.
(*You're getting completely out of control.*)
DAUGHTER: You never ask.
(*It's none of your business.*)

In the second version, the thoughts are given not as simple statements but in the form of an interior dialogue between two voices. The result is richer because it is more complex.

MOTHER: I knew something like this would happen.
(*The silly fool was heading for something like this . . . Not if you'd*

been paying her a bit more attention . . . But I've been so busy at work – she's old enough to know better.)

DAUGHTER: What do you mean?

(*Is that all she can say . . . Why don't you say something, say sorry.*)

MOTHER: You're going to have to tell your father when he comes home.

(*Why come out with that old cliché? . . . He should be stricter with her . . . You know it's not his fault – he gets on better with her.*)

DAUGHTER: What do you mean, 'you knew'?

(*I don't want her talking about him . . . You should talk about him . . .*)

MOTHER: You never tell us where you're going or what you're doing.

(*You can't put all the blame on her . . . She should tell us . . . You never talk to her.*)

DAUGHTER: You never ask.

(*Why not talk to her properly . . . I can't, she wouldn't listen.*)

Sub-text is not just expression of private thoughts but can also refer to communication of intended meaning. The meaning of the exchange will depend on the context; the degree to which it will be understood by the participants and audience may vary which adds to the complexity of the communication. The following example shows how a sub-text can be created which indicates, not so much the unspoken thoughts of the speaker, but the thoughts of the person to whom the dialogue is being directed. The emphasis here is on the way the communication is being received, although they are still written in first person form.

None of these shirts is ironed.

(*Why aren't you doing your proper job as a wife?*)

It's still plugged in downstairs.

(*Do it yourself – I'm not a slave.*)

I've got a really important meeting today.

(*I'm the one who brings the money in – the least you can do is help.*)

I'll probably tidy another cupboard.

(*I wish I had some fulfilment and interest in my life.*)

I'll be late tonight.

(*I'm annoyed with you.*)

Fine.

(*I'm annoyed with you.*)

Exploration of the boundaries, testing the limits of the art form, is a way of educating pupils in dramatic art.

CHAPTER TWENTY-FIVE

Voices

WHISPERERS:	*Salieri! . . . Salieri! . . . Salieri!*
	Salieri! . . . Salieri! . . . Salieri!
VENTICELLO 1:	I don't believe it.
VENTICELLO 2:	I don't believe it.
VENTICELLO 1:	I don't believe it.
VENTICELLO 2:	I don't believe it.
WHISPERERS:	*Salieri!*
VENTICELLO 1:	They say.
VENTICELLO 2:	I hear.
VENTICELLO 1:	I hear.
VENTICELLO 2:	They say.
VENTICELLO 1 and 2:	*I don't believe it!*
WHISPERERS:	*Salieri!*
VENTICELLO 1:	The whole city is talking.
VENTICELLO 2:	You hear it all over.
VENTICELLO 1:	The cafés.
VENTICELLO 2.	The Opera.
VENTICELLO 1:	The Prater.
VENTICELLO 2.	The gutter.

Peter Shaffer, *Amadeus*

* * *

FIRST DROWNED: Remember me, Captain?

CAPTAIN CAT: You're Dancing Williams!

FIRST DROWNED: I lost my step in Nantucket.

SECOND DROWNED: Do you see me, Captain? the white bone talking? I'm Tom–Fred the donkeyman . . . we shared the same girl once . . . her name was Mrs Probert . . .

WOMAN'S VOICE: Rosie Probert, thirty three Duck Lane. Come on up,
boys, I'm dead.

Dylan Thomas, *Under Milk Wood*

*   *   *

Enter the Ghosts of RIVERS, GREY, *and* VAUGHAN.

RIVERS: *(To Richard)* Let me sit heavy on thy soul tomorrow,
Rivers, that died at Pomfret! despair, and die!
GREY: (To *Richard*) Think upon Grey, and let thy soul despair!
VAUGHAN: *(To Richard)* Think upon Vaughan, and with guilty fear,
Let fall thy lance: despair, and die!
ALL: *(To Richmond)* Awake, and think our wrongs in Richard's bosom
Will conquer him! awake, and win the day!

Enter the Ghost of HASTINGS.

GHOST: *(To Richard)* Bloody and guilty, guiltily awake,
And in a bloody battle end thy days!
Think on Lord Hastings: despair, and die!
(To Richmond) Quiet untroubled soul, awake, awake!
Arm, fight, and conquer, for fair England's sake!

Enter the ghosts of the two young PRINCES.

GHOSTS: *(To Richard)* Dream on thy cousins smother'd in the Tower:
Let us be lead within thy bosom, Richard,
And weigh thee down to ruin, shame, and death!
Thy nephews' souls bid thee despair and die!
(To Richmond) Sleep, Richmond, sleep in peace, and wake in joy;
Good angels guard thee from the boar's annoy!
Live, and beget a happy race of kings!
Edward's unhappy sons do bid thee flourish.

William Shakespeare, *King Richard The Third*

*   *   *

Seven years and the summer is over
Seven years since the Archbishop left us,
He who was always kind to his people.
But it would not be well if he should return.
King rules or barons rule;
We have suffered various oppression,

But mostly we are left to our own devices,
And we are content if we are left alone.

T.S. Eliot, Murder in the Cathedral

Commentary

Each of these extracts uses the technique of 'disembodied' voices to contribute to the mood and meaning of the drama. In each case the voices belong to specific figures in the play but the level of interaction with each other or with other characters is limited or non-existent.

The first text is from the opening section of Shaffer's play, *Amadeus*. The stage directions indicate that at the start of the performance all is in darkness as whispers fill the theatre – the words 'Salieri' and 'Assassin' are hissed with increasing intensity. The start of *Amadeus* has a number of interesting features as a beginning to a play (see Chapter 3): the use of flashback technique (we first see the main protagonist Salieri as an old man near death), the revelation of the outcome of the plot which affects the nature of the play's tension (we are given information right from the start that the play will centre on Salieri's involvement in Mozart's death), the use of a chorus as commentary on the action. For the purpose of this chapter, however, it is the use of voices which is of most significance.

The stage directions indicate that the Venticelli, who are the purveyors of fact, rumour and gossip throughout the play, speak extremely rapidly 'so that the scene has the air of a dreadful Overture'. As Innes (1992: 414) has commented, 'Described by Shaffer in musical terms as a fantasia, *Amadeus* is conceived as an opera . It is framed by an overture and a final coda, in which the orchestral qualities of the dialogue are particularly clear, with the massed citizens as a chorus accompanying the solo voices of the two Venticelli.' The voices contribute significantly to the dark mood which pervades the beginning of the play.

Dylan Thomas' *Under Milk Wood* is sub-titled 'a play for voices' and was originally written for the radio. It departs from the normal convention of dialogic, conversational exchanges in favour of creating meaning by interweaving voices. Some of the voices do engage in dialogue, but from others come songs and narratives. The technique allows the author to penetrate and articulate the dreams of the characters at the start of the play as they lie in bed. This in turn allows the time to switch with ease to the past and back to the present again; some of the voices are those of the dead. As Williams (1952: 245) has commented, the use of voices means that 'the reach of the drama is significantly enlarged'.

In Shakespeare's play King Richard is asleep in his tent on Bosworth field before his final battle. In his dreams appear the ghosts of his victims in the precise order in which they met their deaths by his hand. The opposing army is camped nearby (a convention which the audience must accept) and the voices are also able to speak to the Earl of Richmond who will eventually conquer and succeed Richard. The ghosts enter in turn to accuse him, and serve both as a reminder of his past cruelties and an expression of his troubled conscience.

The voices in *Murder in the Cathedral* are those of the women of Canterbury who operate as a chorus within the play. As with the tradition of chorus in Greek drama, they present expository information (as in this short extract), contribute to the mood of tension and expectancy and emphasise the ritual element in the play (see Chapter 22). The poetry of their verse creates strong visual images which evoke the seasons, time passing and locations which are outside the immediate setting of the drama. They comment on the action but also are central to the theme because they capture the essential progression of Beckett towards martyrdom as they themselves move from passivity to greater involvement in the events which unfold. At the start of the play they declare, 'And we are content if we are left alone', whereas in the final speech they admit their involvement, 'We acknowledge our trespass, our weakness, our fault'.

Apart from the aside, soliloquy or monologue, the language of most drama consists of dialogue between characters. I have used the category 'voices' to refer to those times in a play when not only is there no significant conversational exchange but also the utterances are largely removed from any significant action. As with narrative, the use of voices seems to depart from the central ingredient of dramatic action which is normally realised in the tension and conflict created through exchanges between characters. However, the use of the convention can create mood, widen the sphere of reference, move outside the limitations of naturalistic dialogue and fulfil a symbolic function. Because the use of voices does not have to rely on other signing systems in drama, its use with pupils can be quite straightforward, once the initial feeling of strangeness is overcome.

Examples

The following examples correspond to the different ways in which the convention is used by dramatists in the extracts:
• as a way of initiating drama
• as a central device in the construction of the drama

- to represent a character's conscience as in a dream
- as a chorus commenting on the action.

A play about a life story of an old person or someone living on the streets can begin with pupils voicing the thoughts of the character as he or she nears death (*Starting Drama Teaching*, 1994:). These emerge in random fashion and, as in *Under Milk Wood*, speech, hopes, dreams, snatches of conversation, accusations can all be voiced, blending the real and the imaginary. This activity can constitute a starting point for the drama which may then go on to explore the person's life story. However it is more effective if the initial exercise is itself treated theatrically rather than simply as a brainstorm activity. For example, the character in question whose voices are being heard can establish his/her presence by a brief piece of framing action (settling down on a park bench, feeding the birds and then nodding off to sleep). The voices which surround the character should vary in volume and rhythm, some coaxing, some accusatory. They can be articulated spontaneously at first in order to explore possible ideas for the creation of the drama but can then be selected and revised for more polished presentation.

In a drama about a village which is facing a crisis (the possible eruption of a volcano nearby, an attack by a neighbouring tribe, a disease which is rapidly spreading through the community) the voices of a past generation are heard when a similar crisis was threatening many years previously. The use of voices in this way does not have to be explained in terms of the dramatic plot but serves to add texture and depth to the drama which is unfolding, creating a sense of history for the community. However some groups may find it difficult to cope with such a departure from naturalism and may accept the convention more readily if an explanation is built in to the play. For example, the voices can be taken to articulate the letters, journals and other writings of the previous generation which have been consulted for advice on the current crisis.

Alternatively in a village drama the voices at night may simply represent the dreams of the characters as they sleep. This approach draws fairly directly on *Under Milk Wood* in which the dreams of the sleeping villagers express their memories of former friends, childhood memories, present relationships. Fantasy bordering on the surreal quality of dreams can mix with more obvious associations. In this way the relationships, tensions, private concerns and jealousies can be articulated to add impetus to the more naturalistic drama which is being enacted.

In a play based on the theme of bullying the pressure on the victim can be conveyed not just by enacting scenes but through the voices of the perpetrators. Alternatively, the voices of the accusers can be heard at night as the bully sleeps, employing a technique similar to that used in *King Richard The Third*. In the same way a prisoner in a cell can be haunted by the voices of those he has hurt, including victims and family he has left behind.

O'Neill (1995: 86) describes the use of disembodied voices in a drama based on an Irish folk tale *The Seal Wife*. The story tells of a young fisherman who sees a beautiful woman on the shore don a skin and become a seal. By stealing the skin he forces her to stay, marry him and bear his children. I do not propose to summarise the full details of the sessions which can be read in *Drama Worlds*. What is interesting however is that at various points in the project the participants become

• the voices of members of the community whispering their opinions and rumours about the seal wife;
• a collage of voices of children speaking as they wish, retelling stories of the sea told to them by their parents;
• the voices of the seal wife and her children whispering to the fisherman.

The convention is interspersed with other activities including tableaux and improvisation, but the use of voices has particular aesthetic relevance to the dramatisation of a folk tale which has deep roots in a community.

Community is also relevant to the use of voices as chorus because the technique involves an articulation of communal rather than individual utterances. Banks (1991: 19) has pointed out the functional origins of the chorus in Greek drama not just as a way of commenting on the play, but more basically as a way of being heard across the huge distances which separated players from audience. The role of the chorus moreover evolved over time and from one playwright to another and was variously employed as narrator, as commentator on the action, or as a way of introducing pauses and reflection. Aston and Savona (1991: 69) have drawn a contrast between the Greek chorus which 'confirms the values of the community' and the Brechtian use of chorus which 'offers a means of challenging and changing them'. These various insights can be applied to the use of voices as chorus technique when creating classroom drama.

Once a group has taken the plunge of experimenting with form, it is not difficult to determine ways in which a chorus can be introduced into drama. Groups of villagers (concerned about the plague of rats in their homes), neighbours (wondering about the stranger who has moved into their street), and factory workers (unhappy with the working conditions) can all be given communal rather than individual voices. Pupils who may be less confident in participating in the drama may be given a more comfortable role within a group. In *Living With Lady Macbeth* the author, Rob John, used five of the schoolgirl characters as a chorus. They are meant to move and think as one and convey a sinister presence for the main character who is not part of their group. In addition to speaking in chorus, the girls take separate sections of lines so that the whole effect is one of choral speaking:

> THE FIVE GIRLS: (5) What we won't tolerate are the dumb (1) and dumpy (2) the ugly (3) untrendy (4) girls with anoraks (5) and funny-looking parents (1) with glasses (2) and no O levels (3) girls who add nothing to our corporate (4) image and appeal (1) girls (2) in short (3) who are naff (5) like Lily Morgan.

Of all the conventions described in this book 'voices' is perhaps one of the ones which pupils may find it most difficult to adapt to, not because of any intrinsic difficulty with using the technique but because it represents such a departure from naturalistic approaches. It does however represent another means of exploring content and form in drama and may be an indicator of growing confidence and skill in using the art form.

Bibliography

Arts Council of Great Britain (1992) *Drama in Schools* (London: Arts Council).

Aston, A. and Savona, G. (1991) *Theatre as Sign-system* (London: Routledge).

Bain, E., Morris, J. and Smith, R. (eds) (1996) *King Lear* – Cambridge School Shakespeare Edition (Cambridge: Cambridge University Press).

Banks, R. A. (1991) *Drama and Theatre Arts* (London: Hodder and Stoughton).

Bennett, A. (1988) The Introduction to *Talking Heads* (London: BBC Books).

Bentley, E. (ed.) (1968) *The Theory of the Modern Stage* (Harmondsworth: Penguin).

Bevington, D. and Rasmussen, E. (eds) (1993) *Doctor Faustus – Christopher Marlowe and his Collaborator and Revisers* (Manchester: Manchester University Press).

Boal, A. (1992) *Games for Actors and Non-Actors*. Translated by Jackson, A. (London: Routledge).

Bolt, R. (1960) Preface to *A Man for All Seasons* (London: Heinemann Education).

Bolton, G. (1979) *Towards a Theory of Drama in Education* (London: Longman).

Bolton, G. (1984) *Drama as Education* (London: Longman).

Bolton, G. (1992) *New Perspectives on Classroom Drama* (Hemel Hempstead: Simon and Schuster).

Brook, P. (1968) *The Empty Space* (Harmondsworth: Penguin).

Bulman, J. C. (ed.) (1996) *Shakespeare, Theory, and Performance* (London and New York: Routledge).

Burgess, R. and Gaudry, P. (1985) *Time for Drama – A Handbook for Secondary Teachers* (Milton Keynes: Open University Press).

Byron, K. (1986) *Drama in the English Classroom* (London: Methuen).

Carlson, M. (1996) *Peformance: a critical introduction* (London: Routledge).

Cattanach, A.(1992) *Drama for People with Special Needs* (London: A&C Black).

Cooper, D. (1992) *A Companion to Aesthetics* (Oxford: Basil Blackwell).

Counsell, C. (1996) *Signs of Performance* (London: Routledge).

Davies, G. (1983) *Practical Primary Drama* (London: Heinemann).

Davis, D. and Lawrence, C. (1986) *Gavin Bolton: Selected Writings* (London: Longman).

Donoghue, D. (1971) *Yeats* (London: Fontana).

Edwards, F. (1976) *Ritual and Drama* (Guildford and London: Lutterworth Press).

Elam, K. (1980) The Semiotics of Theatre and Drama (London: Methuen). Reprinted in 1988 by Routledge.

Ellis-Fermor, U. (1945) *The Frontiers of Drama* (London: Methuen).
Ellman, R. (1987) *Oscar Wilde* (Harmondsworth: Penguin).
Esslin, M. (1978) *An Anatomy of Drama* (London: Abacus Sphere Books).
Esslin, M. (1987) *The Field of Drama* (London: Methuen).
Fines, J. and Verrier, R. (1974) *The Drama of History* (London: New University Education).
Fleming, M. (1994) *Starting Drama Teaching* (London: David Fulton Publishers).
Frayn, M. (1980) The Introduction to *Chekhov Plays* (London: Methuen).
Goodwin, J. and Taylor, B. (1996) *Solo 1, 2 and 3: Monologues for Drama in English* (London: Hodder and Stoughton).
Griffiths, S. (1982) *How Plays Are Made* (London: Heinemann Education).
Heathcote, D. and Bolton, G. (1995) *Drama for Learning: An Account of Dorothy Heathcote's 'Mantle of the Expert'* (Portsmouth, New Hampshire: Heinemann).
Hooks, E. (1994) *The Ultimate Scene and Monologue Sourcebook* (New York: Back Stage Books).
Hornbrook, D. (1989) *Education and Dramatic Art* (London: Blackwell Education).
Hornbrook, D. (1991) *Education in Drama: Casting the dramatic curriculum* (London: Falmer Press).
Hornbrook, D. (1995) 'Mr. Gargary's Challenge: Reflections on NADIE Journal: International Research Issue' *NADIE Journal,* **19**(1), 78–88.
Innes, C. (1992) *Modern British Drama 1890–1990* (Cambridge: Cambridge University Press).
Johnson, L. and O'Neill, C. (1984). *Dorothy Heathcote: Collected Writings on Education and Drama* (London: Hutchinson).
Jump, J. (1962) The Introduction to *Doctor Faustus* (Manchester: Manchester University Press).
Kempe, A. (1988) *The Drama Sampler* (Oxford: Basil Blackwell).
Kempe. A. (1990) *The GCSE Drama Coursebook* (Oxford: Basil Blackwell).
Kempe, A. (ed.) (1996) *Drama Education and Special Needs* (Cheltenham: Stanley Thornes).
Kitson, N. and Spiby, I. (1996) *Primary Drama Handbook* (London: Watts Books).
Lodge, D. (1992) *The Art of Fiction* (London: Penguin).
Lyons, C. (1983) *Samuel Beckett* (London: Macmillan).
Milne, G. (1986) *The Great Fire of London* (New Barnet, Hertfordshire: Historical Publications Ltd).
Morgan, N. and Saxton, J. (1987) *Teaching Drama* (London: Hutchinson).
Neelands, J. (1990) *Structuring Drama Work* (edited by Goode) (Cambridge: Cambridge University Press).
O'Neill, C. (1995) *Drama Worlds* (Portsmouth, New Hampshire: Heinemann).
O'Neill, C. & Lambert, A. (1982) *Drama Structures: A Practical Handbook for Teachers* (London: Hutchinson).
O'Neill, C., Lambert, A., Linnell, R. and Warr-Wood, J. (1976) *Drama Guidelines* (London: Heinemann).
O'Toole, J. (1992) *The Process of Drama (Negotiating Art and Meaning)* (London: Routledge).
O'Toole, J. and Haseman, B. (1986,7&8) *Dramawise – An Introduction to GCSE Drama* (London: Heinemann).
Pavis, P. (1992) *Theatre at the Crossroads of Culture* (London and New York: Routledge).

Pemberton-Billing, R.and Clegg, J. (1965) *Teaching Drama* (London: University of London Press).

Peter, M. (1994) *Drama For All* (London: David Fulton Publishers).

Peter, M. (1995) *Making Drama Special* (London: David Fulton Publishers).

Pfister, M. (1988) *The Theory and Analysis of Drama* (Cambridge: Cambridge University Press).

Pine, R. (1990) *Brian Friel and Ireland's Drama* (London and New York: Routledge).

Rajan, B. (1965) *W. B. Yeats: A Critical Introduction* (London: Hutchinson).

Rankin, I. (1995) *Drama 5–14, A Practical Approach to Classroom Drama* (London: Hodder and Stoughton).

Readman G. and Lamont, G. (1994) *Drama – A Handbook for Primary Teachers* (London: BBC Education).

Schechner, R. (1993) *The Future of Ritual – Writings on Culture and Performance* (London: Routledge).

Schneider, D. (1949) 'Play of Dreams', *Theatre Arts*, October.

Simner, B. (1994) *Can We Write It As A Play?* (London: Hodder and Stoughton).

States, B. (1994) *The Pleasures of the Play* (United States: Cornell University Press).

Styan, J. L. (1967) *Shakespeare's Stagecraft* (Cambridge: Cambridge University Press).

Styan, J. L. (1975) *Drama, Stage and Audience* (Cambridge: Cambridge University Press).

Szondi, P. (1987) *Theory of the Modern Drama*. Edited and translated by Hays, M. (Cambridge: Polity Press).

Taylor, P. (ed.) (1996) *Researching Drama and Arts Education* (London: Falmer Press).

Wagner, B. J. (1976) *Dorothy Heathcote – Drama as a Learning Medium* (Washington, D.C.: National Education Association).

Welland, D. (1979) *Miller – The Playwright* (London: Methuen).

Williams, R. (1952 and 1973) *Drama from Ibsen to Brecht* (Harmondsworth: Penguin).

Woolland, B. (1993) *The Teaching of Drama in the Primary School* (London: Longman).

Bibliography of Primary Sources

Ayckbourn, *Absurd Person Singular* (London: Penguin) First performed: 1972.

Beckett, *Waiting for Godot* (London: Faber) First performed: 1955.

Bennett, *A Chip in the Sugar* (London: BBC Books) First recorded for television: 1987.

Bolt, *A Man for All Seasons* (London: Heinemann) First performed: 1960.

Brecht, *Galileo* (Indiana University Press) English version by Charles Laughton. First performed in America: 1947.

Chekhov, *Three Sisters* (London: Methuen) Translated by Michael Frayn. This version first performed: 1985.

Churchill, *Top Girls* (London: Methuen) First performed: 1982.

Eliot, *Murder in the Cathedral* (London: Faber) First performed: 1935.

Friel, *Philadelphia, Here I Come* (London: Faber) First performed: 1964.

Galsworthy, *The Silver Box* (London: Duckworth) First performed: 1906.

Ibsen, *Hedda Gabler* (London: Faber) Translated by Christopher Hampton. This version first performed: 1970.

Marlowe, *Dr Faustus* (London: Methuen).

Miller, *Death of a Salesman* (London: Heinemann) First performed in England: 1949.

Miller, *The Crucible* (London: Penguin) First performed in England: 1954.

O'Casey, *The Plough and The Stars* (London: Macmillan) First performed: 1926.

Pinter, *Betrayal* (London: Methuen) First performed: 1978.

Priestley, *An Inspector Calls* (London: Samuel French) First performed: 1946.

Rattigan, *Separate Tables* (London: Methuen) First performed: 1954.

Shaffer, *Amadeus* (London: Penguin) First performed: 1979.

Shaffer, *The Royal Hunt of the Sun* (London: Hamish Hamilton) First performed: 1964.

Shakespeare, *King Richard III*.

Shakespeare, *Macbeth*.

Shakespeare, *A Midsummer Night's Dream*.

Shakespeare, *Othello*.

Sophocles, *King Oedipus* (London: Penguin) Translated by E. F. Watling.

Stoppard, *Rosencrantz and Guildenstern are Dead* (London: Faber) First performed: 1966.

Thomas, *Under Milk Wood* (London: Dent) First broadcast: 1954.

Wertenbaker, *Our Country's Good* (London: Faber) First performed: 1988.

Wilde, *Lady Windermere's Fan* (London: Methuen) First performed: 1892.

Yeats, *On Baile's Strand* in 'Collected Plays' (London: Macmillan) First performed: 1905.

Index